THE FEASTS OF ISRAEL:
SEASONS OF THE MESSIAH

by BRUCE SCOTT

The Friends of Israel Gospel Ministry, Inc.
P. O. Box 908, Bellmawr, NJ 08099

THE FEASTS OF ISRAEL:
SEASONS OF THE MESSIAH

Bruce Scott

Copyright © 1997 by The Friends of Israel Gospel Ministry, Inc.
Bellmawr, New Jersey 08099

Seventh Printing 2010

Library of Congress Catalog Card Number: 96-84008
ISBN-10 0-915540-14-2
ISBN-13 978-0-915540-14-3

Cover by Left Coast Designs, Portland, OR
Artwork by Stan Stein of Stein Arts, Northfield, NJ

Visit our Web site at *www.foi.org*

CONTENTS

DEDICATION

For all of their love and support,
this volume is affectionately dedicated
to my wife Janet
and our two children, Rachel and Reuben.

INTRODUCTION

The feasts of Israel are unequivocally unique.

They are unique because they were established by the Word of God.

They are unique because they belong to a unique people—the Jewish people.

They are unique because they picture and foreshadow the person and work of the promised Messiah.

A study of the feasts or holidays of Israel helps to understand the biblical and historical underpinnings of modern-day Jewish culture. It also helps bring to light an intricate, spiritual tapestry woven by the hand of God, a tapestry illustrating the marvelous plan of salvation that He has designed.

Referred to hundreds of times in Scripture, the holidays of Israel are described as "the feasts of the LORD" (Lev. 23:2), "holy convocations" (Lev. 23:4), "solemn feasts" (Num. 15:3), and "holyday[s]" (Ps 42:4). At the behest of God, they were to be dutifully proclaimed "in their seasons" (Lev. 23:4).

This study attempts to play a part in that proclamation by showing what the festivals are, how they are observed (primarily by Orthodox Jews), how they fit into biblical prophecy, and, finally, how they may be applied to our personal lives. The Jewish calendar and the major festivals will be examined, as well as each of the minor festivals, both biblical and nonbiblical. Throughout the book, key words will be italicized on the first occasion of their use. These words may also be found in the glossary.

The Feasts of Israel: Seasons of the Messiah has been written primarily with Christian readers in mind. Nevertheless, all are welcome to read it. God invites everyone to come and sit at His *spiritual table*, open the *menu*, and discover the sumptuous *feast*

He offers through Jesus the Messiah.

A blessing often recited on Jewish holidays is appropriate for the beginning of this hopefully soul-satisfying repast: "Blessed art thou, O Lord our God, King of the universe, who hast kept us in life, and hast preserved us, and enabled us to reach this season." Amen.

Now, let's partake of our feast from God's Word.

Calendar of Festivals and Fasts of the Jewish year.

Gregorian	Hebrew month	Notable days and observances
Sept.–Oct.	TISHRI	1 Rosh ha-Shanah (New Year); 2 Rosh ha-Shanah (New Year); 3 Fast of Gedaliah; Ten days of Penitence; 10 Yom Kippur (day of Atonement); 15 Sukkot (Tabernacles); 16 –kol-hamo'ed–; 21 Hoshanah Rabba; 22 Shemini Azeret / Simchat Torah; 23 Simchat Torah
Oct.–Nov.	CHESHVAN	—
Nov.–Dec.	KISLEV	25 Hanukkah
Dec.–Jan.	TEVET	10 Fast of Tenth of Tevet
Jan.–Feb.	SHEVAT	15 Tu bi-Shevat
Feb.–Mar.	ADAR	13 Fast of Esther; 14 Purim; 15 Shushan Purim
Mar.–April	NISAN	14 Fast of the firstborn; 15 Pesah (Passover); 16 –kol-hamo'ed–; 21 Pesah last day (Festival); 27 Yom ha-Sho'ah (Day of Holocaust)
April–May	IYYAR	4 Yom Ha-Zikkaron; 5 Yom Ha'atzma'ut (Independence Day); 18 Lag ba-Omer; 28 Yom Yerushalayim
May–June	SIVAN	6 Shavuot (Pentecost)
June–July	TAMMUZ	17 Fast of Seventeenth of Tammuz; Three weeks of Mourning
July–Aug.	AV	Nine Days; 9 Fast of Tishah be-Av; 15 Fifteenth of Av
Aug.–Sept.	Elul	—

Counting of the Omer (Sefirah period) begins (Nisan 16).

Legend

- ■ MAJOR HOLIDAY
- ▦ MINOR HOLIDAY
- ▨ Special day / Holiday in Diaspora only
- ❀ Pilgrimage Festivals
- ✳ Counting of the Omer (Sefirah period) begins
- 1 Simchat Torah in Israel only

1

THE JEWISH CALENDAR

One day I saw a gray hair in my head;
    I plucked it out, when thus to me it said:
"Think, if thou wilt, that thou art rid of me,
    I've twenty friends who soon will mock at thee."[1]

Despite all the creams and ointments that claim otherwise, the aging process cannot be stopped. Time marches on, as they say, and it slows for no one. We are reminded of this adage whenever we turn a page of the calendar. The days and months go as quickly as they come.

The cadence of time's relentless march is set by the sun, moon, and stars. By these celestial bodies we measure time's passing and thus determine our calendar; God has purposed it to be so (Gen. 1:14-19).

Over the centuries numerous cultures have formed their own calendars. The ancient Egyptians, Greeks, and Babylonians each had their own way of reckoning the days, months, and years. Our present calendar is taken from the one established by Pope Gregory XIII in the year 1582. This Gregorian calendar is a solar calendar, as opposed to the lunar calendar, because it is based on the movements of the sun rather than the moon.

Description of the Jewish Calendar

The Jewish people also have their own calendar. It has both lunar and solar components. The months are determined by the moon, the years by the sun. Based on the creation account, the Jewish day begins at sunset with 12 hours of darkness and 12 hours of daylight. When a Jewish holiday is listed on the Gregorian calendar, therefore, the holiday actually begins at sundown the previous evening.

There are 12 months in the Jewish calendar, each consisting of 29 or 30 days. Every second or third year is a leap year in which an extra month is added, thus insuring that the festivals of *Pesach* (Passover), *Shavuot* (Pentecost), and *Sukkot* (Tabernacles) remain in their proper seasons—Pesach in spring, Shavuot in summer, and Sukkot in autumn.

Development of the Jewish Calendar

Since biblical times, the Jewish calendar has retained its essential elements. The seasons are determined by the moon (Ps. 104:19), and there are 12 months (1 Chr. 27:15). Over the years, however, the names of the months have changed, as well as the process by which the calendar is determined or fixed.

Before the Babylonian exile, the Israelites most likely gave their months common Semitic names. After the Babylonian exile, the Jewish calendar evidenced signs of Persian influence. Babylonian names were assigned to the months, and these names are still used in the present-day Jewish calendar.

In addition to the names of the months, the Jewish calendar has changed in yet another way. We may approach the Jewish calendar with great confidence, knowing that it has been determined by precise astronomical calculations. But it has not always been so.

In the days of the *Sanhedrin* (the 71-member governing body of Jewish religious leaders, ca. 63 B.C.- A.D. 425) the calendar was determined each month by the sighting of the new moon. The new moon was important because it established the timing of the observance of the Jewish festivals.

Under the law of Moses, the new moon was marked by blowing two silver trumpets (Num. 10:10) and sacrificing a burnt offering and a sin offering (Num. 28:11–15). Later, the beginning of each month took on additional characteristics. The people feasted (1 Sam. 20:5), closed their businesses (Amos 8:5), and some went to the prophet of God for inquiry and instruction (2 Ki. 4:23).

By the time of the Second Temple, the sighting of the new moon had become a festival in itself. Because only the Sanhedrin in Jerusalem had the authority to set the calendar, the sighting of the new moon was reported to them.

Sumptuous meals were prepared in a large courtyard to encourage the people to serve as witnesses to the sighting. They gathered and waited their turn to be interviewed by the religious leaders. Upon examination of two reliable witnesses, the Sanhedrin declared, "The new month is sanctified—it is sanctified!" The celebration then began. The people were jubilant as the prescribed sacrifices were offered.

Meanwhile, the high priest lifted his hands and blessed the people: "The LORD bless thee, and keep thee; The LORD make his face shine upon thee, and be gracious unto thee; the LORD lift up his contenance upon thee, and give thee peace" (Num. 6:24-26).

The Sanhedrin also gave three blessings: one over the holiday wine; one thanking God for revealing the Jewish calendar; and one expressing the desire that the Messiah come, along with His forerunner, Elijah the prophet.

Today, without the Temple or the Sanhedrin, the new moon holiday, called *Rosh Hodesh* (Head or First of the Month), has changed somewhat. In the synagogue, the date of the forthcoming new moon is announced to the congregation. When the first of the month arrives, a special prayer is recited to replace the Temple sacrifices. There are readings from the *Torah* (Genesis to Deuteronomy, the five books of Moses) and the Psalms. With the blessing of the day, it is customary for each congregant to greet three people with the phrase *Shalom Aleichem* (Peace be unto you), to which the recipients of the greeting reply in reverse terminology, *Aleichem Shalom.*

When Jesus the Messiah returns to the earth, the Scriptures indicate that, with slight modifications, the festival of the new moon will be observed in His kingdom. Appropriate sacrifices will be offered, accompanied by regular worship of God at the Temple (Ezek. 46:6–7). This observance will most likely serve as a memorial, as well as a proper and complete fulfillment of the law of Moses.

In the days of ancient Israel, the celebration of the new moon festival was not to be kept within the confines of Jerusalem. Once the sighting of the new moon had been confirmed, the people were commanded to relay the news from one community to the next, which was accomplished by lighting bonfires atop lookout hills.

Trouble came when the historical Jewish nemesis, the Samaritans, attempted to confuse the Jewish lookouts by lighting their own bonfires at the wrong time of the month. As a result, a new system of communication was developed. Instead of lighting bonfires, trusted and reputable messengers were sent throughout the *Diaspora* (Jewish communities outside of the land of Israel). Although this eliminated the difficulty with the Samaritans, a new problem arose. The messengers were delayed because of the distances between communities, raising doubts as to the proper days on which to observe the appointed festivals. To compensate, the Sanhedrin decreed that Jewish people outside of the land of Israel could celebrate the holidays of Pesach, Shavuot, *Rosh Hashanah* (New Year), and Sukkot for one extra day. Modern Jewry still follows this custom, while Israelis keep the extra day for Rosh Hashanah only.

Out of concern for the Diaspora, the Jewish calendar was later fixed solely by calculations under the leadership of Rabbi Hillel II in the fourth century. By the tenth century, the modern Jewish calendar had fully developed and included the formation of two Jewish calendars.

In Exodus 12:2 God told Moses and Aaron, "This month shall be unto you the beginning of months: it shall be the first month of the year to you." The month spoken of was *Abib* or *Nisan* (Ex. 13:4). By so designating the month of Nisan as the beginning of months, God created a new calendar for the Israelites. They were to reckon time differently from that point onward. The major reason for this change was to highlight their redemption from Egypt. Every new year was to remind them of their God-given freedom from slavery.

The calendar instituted in Exodus 12:2 was Israel's first and was used to determine festivals. By Jesus' day, however, another Jewish calendar was in use for civil affairs. This second calendar began with the month Tishri. The first of Tishri therefore was considered the Jewish civil New Year. It is this second calendar and second New Year (Rosh Hashanah) that Jewish people follow today.

Seasons of the Jewish Calendar

God created the lights in the heavens to reckon not only days and years, but also seasons. The seasons of the land of Israel in biblical times were much the same as they are today—warm, dry summers (Ps. 32:4) and cool, wet winters (Song 2:11). The summer season is from about May to October, and winter is from November to April. While Israel has spring and autumn, the Scriptures refer mainly to the dominant seasons of summer and winter (Ps. 74:17).

During Bible times, the seasons in Israel determined the agricultural activities of sowing and reaping, planting and harvesting. Generally, planting was done in winter months (Prov. 20:4), harvesting in summer months (Prov. 10:5). The crops gathered at the beginning of the harvest season were called "first fruits" (Ex. 23:16). Crops gathered at the end of the harvest season were known as "summer fruit" (Amos 8:2). Two of Israel's major festivals were divinely integrated with the time of harvest. Shavuot (Pentecost) celebrated the beginning of harvest, and Sukkot (Tabernacles) the end (Ex. 23:16).

ENDNOTE

[1] Yehudah Halevi, *A Treasury of Jewish Humor,* ed. Nathan Ausubel (Garden City: Doubleday & Company, Inc., 1951), p. 80.

PART I
THE MAJOR FEASTS

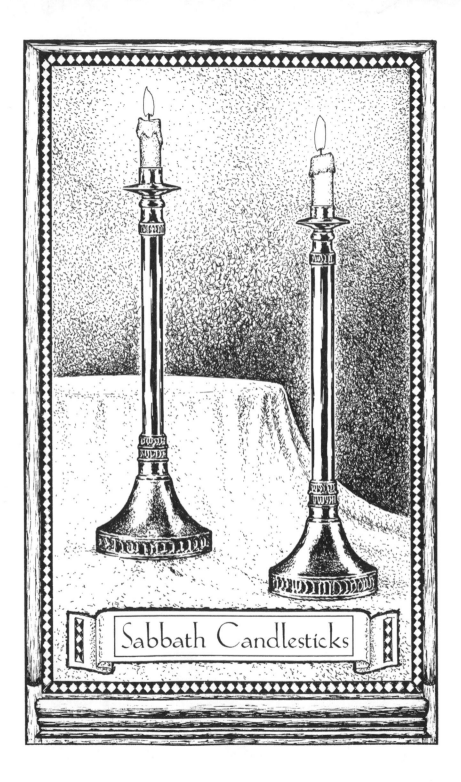

Sabbath Candlesticks

2

SABBATH:
THE DAY OF REST

The table is covered with the finest cloth. Two loaves of *hallah* (holiday bread) lie beneath a lovely piece of embroidered fabric. Sitting atop ornamented candlesticks, two candles await the arrival of the special day. The mother of the family looks anxiously out the window, examining the position of the sun.

"Hurry, children," she calls out. "Put on your nice things. It's getting late. The sun is almost set. The Sabbath is almost here!"

As the family scurries to wash and change into their festive garments—clothing reserved solely for the Sabbath—mother looks around to make sure everything is prepared and in order. Once the Sabbath has begun, no further work is permitted. Everything the family will need during the next 24 hours must be ready before the day of rest begins.

Quickly the children gather at the table, faces scrubbed and hair combed. The father, regally dressed, stands smiling at his little

ones. Mother breathes a sigh of relief and contentment. The pace
slows considerably as she reverently lights the Sabbath candles.
She waves her hands over and around the flames then covers her
eyes and recites the traditional blessing, officially welcoming the
honored guest, the Sabbath Queen. The day of rest, with its
accompanying joy, may now begin.

This scene, taken from the motion picture *Fiddler on the Roof*,
has been repeated for centuries in Jewish homes around the
world. It exemplifies the most beloved of all of Israel's holidays.
Other Jewish festivals come only once a year, but the Sabbath
Queen or Bride, as the day is anthropomorphically called, comes
every seven days and is wed to the people of Israel.

In Jewish tradition, the Sabbath is believed to be a gift from
God's treasury. Exalted and elevated, it is the day held to be the
foundation and epitome of Jewish faith. It is revered and almost
worshiped. The Sabbath is so important that it is looked on as
being the primary instrument by which the Jewish people have
been sustained and preserved throughout the ages. As one Jewish
thinker said, "More than the Jews have kept the Sabbath, the
Sabbath has kept the Jews."[1]

Origin and Description of the Sabbath

The Hebrew word *Shabbat* (Sabbath) comes from a word
meaning to *desist, cease,* or *rest.* In the Bible, Sabbath primarily
speaks of the seventh day of the week, the day on which God rested or ceased from His creation work (Ex. 20:8-11). There are
actually a number of Sabbaths referred to in the Scriptures. As
already mentioned, there is the Sabbath of every seven days.
There is also a Sabbath on the first day of the seventh month (Lev.
23:23-25). Every seven years the actual land of Israel was to
have a Sabbath or rest and lie fallow (Lev. 25:3-4). Every seven
cycles of seven years was to be followed with a fiftieth year of

Jubilee, during which slaves were set free from their labors and the land again enjoyed rest (Lev. 25:8-11). Finally, the major Jewish festivals—Passover (Unleavened Bread), Shavuot (Pentecost), Rosh Hashanah (Trumpets), *Yom Kippur* (Day of Atonement), and Sukkot (Tabernacles)—were characterized by days of rest (Lev. 23).

The Sabbath day of rest is the first of the holy convocations God bestowed upon the nation of Israel (Lev. 23:3). It was a holy day, set apart because God Himself had blessed the seventh day and sanctified it (Gen. 2:3). Keeping the sanctity or holiness of the Sabbath therefore was highly emphasized in Scripture and was part of the original Ten Commandments. The purpose of the Sabbath was threefold.

First, the Sabbath was to be a day of rest and refreshment for the Israelites, their servants, their livestock, and any visitors staying with them (Dt. 5:13-14). For six days they were to labor, but on the seventh day they were to have a complete rest or cessation from work. In so doing, observant Jews identified with their God, who also worked for six days and rested on the seventh.

Second, the Sabbath was to be a sign between the Lord and Israel (Ex. 31:13). Similar to the sign of circumcision, the Sabbath was to be kept throughout their generations as a sign of the covenant between God and Israel. The penalty for not keeping the Sabbath was the same as that for failure to practice circumcision. Nonobservers were cut off from the covenant people. God gave the sign of the Sabbath so that Israel would know that He, the Lord, sanctified them.

Third, the Sabbath was to be a day of remembering their physical redemption (Dt. 5:15). The people of Israel were not to forget that they had been slaves in Egypt and that God had delivered them with great power and might.

Resting on the seventh day therefore involved more than just physical refreshment. God did not rest on the seventh day because He was fatigued. Rather, the idea of resting spoke more of cessation. The Israelites were to cease whatever work they were engaged in during the week. They were to detach themselves from the material, temporal, and mundane and focus on the spiritual, eternal, and heavenly facets of life. They were to refresh the inner man as well as the outer. They were to reflect on their relationship with God, putting aside their own desires and putting God's desires first (Isa. 58:13-14). By keeping the Sabbath in this way, the Israelites marked out a distinction or division between themselves and the godless world system around them. This is what God intended for Israel when He instituted the Sabbath.

Rabbinical Judaism, however, has added more to the meaning and purpose of the Sabbath. It teaches that the seventh day of rest was not a result of God's ceasing from His work of creation. Rather, God's work was actually finished with the creation of the Sabbath on the seventh day. Jewish tradition also teaches that the Sabbath is equal in itself to all the other commandments found in the Bible. Therefore, keeping the Sabbath is like keeping all of the biblical commands at the same time. Furthermore, whenever observant Jews keep the Sabbath, they believe they are endowed with an additional soul for the duration of the day of rest. At the conclusion of the Sabbath, that extra soul leaves. This additional soul is given so that they may experience and enjoy the spiritual delights of the Sabbath in all of their fullness.

Rabbinical Judaism decided that if keeping the Sabbath meant ceasing from all labor, they must determine what should be classified as work. The Bible gives only a few examples of prohibited activity, such as gathering sticks (Num. 15:32), treading wine presses (Neh. 13:15), and carrying loads (Jer. 17:21). But the biblical concept of work also seems to imply transacting business, earning a living, or working at a professional occupation. Resting on the Sabbath therefore meant that the Israelites were to cease activities centering around their own personal interests and to involve themselves in seeking God's interests.

The rabbinical concept of labor, however, has a much broader definition. An act of work in Rabbinical Judaism is that which "shows man's mastery over the world by the constructive exercise of his intelligence and skill."[2] Based on that definition, the ancient rabbis formulated a list of 39 general categories of work that are prohibited on the Sabbath.

1. Plowing	2. Sowing
3. Reaping	4. Sheaf-making
5. Threshing	6. Winnowing
7. Selecting	8. Sifting
9. Grinding	10. Kneading
11. Baking	12. Sheep-Shearing
13. Bleaching	14. Combing raw materials
15. Dyeing	16. Spinning
17. Weaving operations	18. Weaving operations
19. Weaving operations	20. Separating into threads
21. Tying a knot	22. Untying a knot
23. Sewing	24. Tearing
25. Trapping or hunting	26. Slaughtering
27. Skinning	28. Tanning
29. Scraping pelts	30. Marking (or scoring lines on a surface)
31. Cutting to shape	32. Writing
33. Erasing	34. Building
35. Demolishing	36. Kindling a fire
37. Extinguishing (a fire)	38. The final hammer-blow (putting the finishing touch to a newly manufactured article)
39. Carrying from the private to the public domain (and vice versa)[3]	

These 39 prohibited activities are part of the Oral Law of Judaism. Believed by Jewish teachers to have been given to Moses on Mount Sinai along with the written law, these oral laws, eventually transcribed, hold equal status and authority with the written law.

Because the ancient sages knew the tendency of people to be forgetful, they put safeguards into the Sabbath laws and traditions, known as "erecting a fence around the law." The concept behind this was that if people concentrated on not breaking the "fence" laws, they would not inadvertently break the central laws.

For example, the oral law demands that no plowing be done on the Sabbath. This is a general restriction that, according to rabbinical explanation, includes such actions as "digging; fertilizing the soil; removing stones from the soil; [and] leveling the ground." To safeguard even these activities, the "fence" laws prohibited even further actions, such as "strewing sand or ashes on the ground without leveling," or "sweeping the floor with a hard broom."

Jewish tradition also teaches that grinding includes the acts of "milling or grinding corn, coffee, or pepper; filing metals; [and] pounding or crushing substances in a mortar." The "fence" law therefore prohibits one "to prepare medicine, to take medicine, and to carry out any treatment, for the relief of discomfort or pain or slight ailments (since to do these things is habitually connected with the pounding of medicinal ingredients). The ['fence' law] does not apply in cases of acute pain or actual illness [or when the patient's life is in danger]."[4]

Along with the 39 categories of work, the rabbis also amplified the biblical charge to Israel of abiding in their private domains on the Sabbath (Ex. 16:29). It was decided that people could journey a distance of 2,000 cubits (a little more than half a mile) from their hometowns or cities without breaking the commandment.

In ancient days, this distance was actually measured by designated surveyors. (This is probably why it was known that the Mount of Olives was within the limits of a Sabbath day's journey [Acts 1:12].) However, to protect those who erred in crossing the Sabbath limit, the surveyors shortened the 2,000-cubit limit by about 15 cubits.

Determining the limits of private and public domain was also crucial in order to avoid breaking the prohibition of carrying a load on the day of rest. It is against Sabbath law to carry an item from a person's private domain into the public domain. This includes even such cursory things as a house key or a piece of paper. A whole tractate in the *Talmud* is dedicated to this problem and how to work around it. The solution agreed upon was to increase the size of a person's private domain and extend its limits, which was accomplished through the *eruv* (lit., *mixture*). The eruv was a portion of food prepared ahead of time and placed strategically at the 2,000-cubit Sabbath limit. The location of the eruv was then considered a place of temporary abode—a private domain—enabling a person to travel an additional 2,000 cubits from that spot without breaking the Sabbath law.

The eruv was also used as an arrangement between neighbors. By depositing a portion of food, such as a loaf of bread or a piece of *matzo* (unleavened bread), at a certain site, all parties involved in the agreement were entitled to unlimited access to each other's homes since all of the dwellings in question were considered as one large private domain.

The modern version of the eruv takes the form of a polyurethane or nylon cord, symbolizing the walls and doorways of a private domain. This cord is stretched across the tops of utility poles marking out the boundaries of the private domain. Many large cities with significant Jewish populations have eruv cords, some encompassing huge sections of the metropolitan area.

The penalty for breaking the Sabbath was severe. The Lord declared, "whosoever doeth any work in the sabbath day, he shall surely be put to death" (Ex. 31:15). The rabbis understood this to mean that if people profaned the Sabbath unintentionally, they were required to bring a sin offering to the Temple. If, after a warning, witnesses saw them again breaking the Sabbath, the penalty was death by stoning (Num. 15:36), because their acts were done intentionally and out of defiance of the Sabbath law.

A devastating penalty was meted out to the children of Israel in Old Testament days. As God had promised, because they had not kept the required seven-year Sabbath rest for the land, they were expelled from the land and taken captive by their enemies. Later they returned, but only after the land had enjoyed the number of Sabbaths it had previously been denied (2 Chr. 36:21).

Observance of the Sabbath

The weekly Sabbath is observed from sunset on Friday to sunset on Saturday. According to Scripture, the children of Israel are required to observe it throughout their generations (Ex. 31:16). However, apart from the Orthodox Jews, few within the Jewish community observe the Sabbath with any consistency.

In biblical times, those who worked in the Temple were exempt from the Sabbath requirements, as is obvious from Scripture. The Temple sacrifices did not cease on the Sabbath, nor did other priestly duties, such as changing the showbread (Lev. 24:8). A unique aspect of the Temple activities on the Sabbath was the addition of two more sacrifices to the daily whole burnt offering (Num. 28:9-10). Also, the Sabbath was the only holy convocation given to Israel on which no sin offering was required. Furthermore, on the Sabbath the Levites chanted a specific Psalm, as they did for every day of the week. On the Sabbath they recited Psalm 92. Believing that it contained a prophetic, futuristic aspect, they understood that Psalm as looking ahead to the messianic age, a time that was to be "all Sabbath and rest in the life everlasting."[5]

Preparation for the Sabbath has always been important in the Jewish community (see Mk. 15:42). The Sabbath is looked upon as the culmination of the week. The entire week looks forward to the seventh day. Anticipation increases as the week progresses. Finally, as the time draws near, Jewish businesses close early to give the employees sufficient time to make preparations. In Israel public services, such as buses, also cease operation. According to Jewish teaching, preparations for the Sabbath should begin with the attitude that a royal guest is coming to dinner, a guest called "Queen Sabbath." In fact, in the synagogue the commencement of the Sabbath is greeted with the words, "Come, my Beloved, to meet the Bride, Queen Sabbath."[6]

Preparations continue with the turning on of the lights. Since electricity is viewed as a form of fire, turning on a lamp would be breaking the rule against lighting a fire. Therefore, all lamps must be lit before sundown. To get around this inconvenience, some Jewish families use electrical timers that switch the lights on and off automatically.

A similar problem exists with food preparation. Jewish law does not allow cooking on the Sabbath. But people have to eat. Therefore, two things are done. First, much of the Sabbath food is prepared in advance. This was done even in the first century. Second, a "Sabbath stove" is readied. Its burner controls are covered, and the food and necessary liquids are placed on the adjusted burners just before the Sabbath begins. The food cooks, but no person performs a cooking activity.

Other preparations include changing into the best clothes, covering the table with a fancy tablecloth, using the finest china and silverware, and setting out the candles, wine, and Sabbath bread.

In Second Temple days, after all the preparations were completed, the priests sounded the shofar indicating that the Sabbath had begun and all work must cease.

Modern Sabbath prohibitions include fasting, mourning, driving, or any activity associated with business. The only work activity permitted on the Sabbath is circumcision, because of the symbolic significance circumcision holds in becoming a member of the covenant people.

Some Jewish families try to circumvent the Sabbath prohibitions by hiring Gentiles to perform necessary tasks, such as turning on the heat in cold weather. Others believe it is wrong to employ a Gentile in this way.

Once all the work has ceased and all the preparations have been made, it is time for the celebration of the Sabbath to begin. The mother of the family prepares to light the two Sabbath candles, a ritual that is performed at least 18 minutes before sunset on Friday night. According to Jewish tradition, it is the woman's responsibility to light the candles because it was a woman— Eve—who put out the light of man's soul. Before the lighting, it is customary to put coins in a box designated for charity. The mother then lights the candles, covers her eyes, and pronounces the appropriate blessing, inaugurating the Sabbath. Unlike other Jewish holidays, the blessing is spoken *after* the candle lighting. Great importance is placed on the lighting of the Sabbath candles. According to a Jewish legend, God instructed Moses that if Israel lit the Sabbath candles, they would enjoy the light of God's glory in the world to come.

Following the lighting of the candles, the family adjourns to the synagogue, where the service begins. Prayers and Scripture passages are narrated, followed by the *kiddush* (sanctification) blessing over a cup of wine. Following the evening service, it is customary to have an *Oneg Shabbat* (Delight [in the] Sabbath) gathering, where there is singing, discussion of the service, and refreshments. The worshipers depart with a farewell of *Gut Shabes* (Good Sabbath) or *Shabbat Shalom* (Sabbath Peace).

Upon arriving home, it is customary for the parents to bless their children. To the boys they say, "God make thee as Ephraim and as Manasseh" (Gen. 48:20), and to the girls, "God make thee as Sarah, Rebekah, Rachel, and Leah." To both the boys and girls the parents recite the blessing found in Numbers 6:24-26. The father follows this with an expression of praise for his wife. Reciting Proverbs 31:10-31, he extols her in the presence of his children.

Using Genesis 2:1-3, a kiddush is recited over wine, then the two hallah loaves are uncovered, and a blessing is said over them. With the blessing and breaking of the holiday bread, the first of three Sabbath meals (one on Sabbath evening and two the next day) begins. The Sabbath meals are happy occasions with good food, lively conversation, and singing of table songs and hymns. One popular hymn is as follows:

> Mercy, O Rock, for thy people!
> Pity the place of thy glory,
> Zion, the house of our beauty.
> Soon shall he come to redeem us—
> Offspring of David, thy servant,
> He that is breath of our spirit—
> Send thine anointed [lit., Messiah], O Lord![7]

Another synagogue service is conducted on Saturday morning. Along with numerous prayers and hymns, the Torah scroll containing the five books of Moses is read. A different portion is read each Sabbath. Following the Torah reading is a reading from the Prophets.

After the Torah scroll is returned to the depository, it is

common for the rabbi to deliver a sermon. In the first century, visitors were sometimes permitted to make brief comments to the congregation (cp. Acts 13:15–42). Following additional prayers, the morning gathering ends with another kiddush recited over wine.

The second meal at home is followed by a restful afternoon. Some take naps, go for short walks, or study Jewish laws and customs (as was done in Temple days). Later there is an afternoon service at the synagogue with more prayers and readings from Jewish sages and moralists. The family then enjoys another light meal at home and later returns to the synagogue for the concluding evening service.

Sabbath observers regret to see this special day come to an end. Back at home they conduct a last ritual—the *havdalah* (*separation* or *distinction*)—to say good-bye to the Sabbath Queen. Using a spice box, a braided candle, and a cup of wine, they say the following prayer: "Blessed art thou, O Lord our God, King of the universe, who makest a distinction between holy and profane, between light and darkness, between Israel and the heathen nations, between the seventh day and the six working days. Blessed art thou, O Lord, who makest a distinction between holy and profane."[8]

As the havdalah concludes, the Sabbath Queen departs, and a renewed anticipation for her arrival the following week begins.

Prophecy and the Sabbath

The Sabbath is spoken of in the Scriptures more than any other Jewish holiday. Its importance, therefore, to prophetic studies cannot be underestimated, especially as it relates to the coming of the Messiah. It is no wonder that in the New Testament, Jesus of Nazareth did much of His teaching and miracles on the Sabbath, using the occasion to give further evidence of His messianic credentials.

On a number of Sabbaths, Jesus chose to miraculously heal several people suffering from various illnesses. Of course, all of these healings broke the commonly accepted rabbinical interpretations of Sabbath law. As has already been seen, unless a life is in danger or in cases of acute pain, the practice of healing is not allowed on the Sabbath. This position is exemplified by the synagogue official's reaction in Luke 13:14. Indignant over Jesus' healing on the Sabbath, he said to the crowd, "There are six days in which men ought to work; in them, therefore, come and be healed, and not on the sabbath day." This regulation apparently was commonly known by the people. Mark 1:32-34 specifies that the people waited to come to Jesus to be healed until "the sun did set." If so many were in such need, why did they wait until after the sun had set—the start of a new day on the Jewish calendar—to come and be healed? The answer is that Jewish law forbade them to receive medical attention on the Sabbath.

It should be clarified that Jesus was not *anti-Sabbath*. In fact, the Bible records that it was "his custom" (Lk. 4:16) to attend synagogue on the Sabbath day. But through His healing efforts, Jesus went against the grain of numerous Sabbath rules. By mixing dirt and spittle to make salve for the blind man in John 9, Jesus broke the Sabbath law against preparing mixtures for medicinal purposes. Some of the Pharisees responded, "This man is not of God, because he keepeth not the sabbath day" (Jn. 9:16).

By saying to the disabled man of Bethesda, "Rise, take up thy bed, and walk" (Jn. 5:8), Jesus bid him to break the Sabbath law against carrying. The Jewish leaders said to the cured man, "It is the sabbath day; it is not lawful for thee to carry thy bed" (Jn. 5:10).

Jesus Himself also broke the Sabbath law against carrying. Matthew 8:17 points out that by healing so many people of their diseases, Jesus fulfilled the messianic prophecy of Isaiah 53:4: "He himself took our infirmities, and bore [or carried] our sicknesses." Therefore, Jesus broke Jewish law by carrying something on the Sabbath day—namely, our sicknesses.

By healing the crippled woman in Luke 13, Jesus broke several Sabbath laws. The *Mishnah* states that one "may not straighten a [deformed] child's body or set a broken limb"[9] on the Sabbath. Although this law may not have applied to this woman, He set her body aright on the Sabbath.

Jesus also was culpable within Sabbath law because by healing this bent-over woman, He had in effect *untied* a knot. He was aware of this, as indicated by His statement in Luke 13:16: "ought not this woman, being a daughter of Abraham, whom Satan hath bound, lo, these eighteen years, be loosed from this bond on the sabbath day?" The Greek word for *loosed* used here literally means *released* or *untied*. Jesus *untied* a knot by healing this woman.

If Jesus had healed her with just one hand, the charge against Him may not have been made, for the Mishnah states, "None is culpable because of any knot which can be untied with one hand."[10] However, Jesus wanted to make a point with His actions and healed the woman using both hands: "And he laid his *hands* on her; and immediately she was made straight, and glorified God" (Lk. 13:13).

In all probability, just a few minutes before Jesus healed this woman who had been bowed over for 18 years, the entire synagogue congregation had uttered a Sabbath benediction still used today: "The Lord slumbereth not, nor sleepeth; He arouseth the sleepers and awakeneth the slumberers; He maketh the dumb to speak, setteth free the prisoners, supporteth the falling, and *raiseth up those who are bowed down.*"[11]

On another occasion Jesus and His disciples broke the Sabbath laws against reaping, threshing, and perhaps grinding. Luke 6:1 states, "And it came to pass, on the second sabbath after the first, that he went through the fields of grain; and his disciples plucked the ears of grain, and did eat, rubbing them in their hands." Certain Pharisees took exception to this. "Why do ye that which is not lawful to do on the sabbath days?" (Lk. 6:2), they asked.

The reaction to Jesus' nonconformity with Sabbath precepts was varied. All were amazed (Mk. 1:27); most were intrigued (Lk. 4:36); some rejected Him (Lk. 4:16-30); and, unfortunately, a few wanted to kill Him. John 5:18 records that the Jewish leaders "sought the more to kill him, because he not only had broken [lit., repealed, annulled, or abolished] the sabbath, but said also that God was his Father, making himself equal with God."

If Jesus knew that the stakes for breaking the Sabbath were so high, why did He take the risk? A study of the passages dealing with Jesus and the Sabbath reveals certain principles that help to answer this question.

First, through His miraculous life and ministry (such as healing on the Sabbath), Jesus fulfilled specific prophecies proving that He was Israel's long-awaited Messiah.

Second, as the Messiah, Jesus had the authority to supersede the Sabbath. This was not contrary to Jewish tradition. In fact, it was taught that in the days of the Messiah a new Torah would be given to Israel. The idea in both biblical and rabbinic theology is that when the Messiah is present, the law takes a subservient role—a *back seat*, if you will—to Him. Therefore, as the Messiah, Jesus had the right to make such statements as "the Son of man [a messianic title] is Lord even of the sabbath day" (Mt. 12:8).

Third, as the Messiah, Jesus had the authority to correct, reinterpret, and even change the Sabbath laws. On four occasions He demonstrated that overriding Sabbath law had precedence and was not new with Him. He related the biblical story of David and his hungry men eating consecrated showbread reserved only for the priests (Mt. 12:3-4). Although it is not recorded as having occurred on the Sabbath, the action was still a breach of the letter of the law. Jesus also pointed out that on every Sabbath the priests on the Temple Mount broke the laws against working, and yet God considered them blameless (Mt. 12:5). Further, rabbinical rules allowed for the Sabbath to be overriden to perform circumcision (Jn. 7:22-23). Finally, the rabbis allowed the care and well-being of livestock and animals to supplant the Sabbath laws (Mt. 12:11; see also Talmud, Shabbath 117b).

Having exposed the fact that superseding the Sabbath had precedence, Jesus challenged His critics with new ideas: If the Temple and its services are greater than the Sabbath, was not He, as the Messiah, also superior to the Sabbath? As He said, "in this place is one greater than the temple" (Mt. 12:6). And again, "If a man on the sabbath day receive circumcision, that the law of Moses should not be broken, are ye angry with me, because I have made a man entirely well on the sabbath day?" (Jn. 7:23). Finally, if the Jewish leaders went to the trouble of breaking the Sabbath for the benefit of mere animals, why were they so upset when Jesus did it on behalf of a human being? As the Lord put it, "How much, then, is a man better than a sheep?" (Mt. 12:12).

The primary difference between the rabbinical Sabbath and the Sabbath presented by Jesus Christ can be brought down to one statement. Jesus declared, "The sabbath was made for man, and not man for the sabbath" (Mk. 2:27). Although their intentions were good, the rabbis turned the Sabbath into a legalistic burden, not a day of rest. In this man-made system, people and their needs were relegated to second place behind rituals and even animals, which is why the Lord Jesus rebuked His accusers. "If ye had known what this meaneth, I will have mercy, and not sacrifice, ye would not have condemned the guiltless" (Mt. 12:7).

In contrast to the rabbinical system, Jesus, as the Messiah, understood that people and their needs were always first in God's sight. He said, "Wherefore, it is lawful to do good on the sabbath days" (Mt. 12:12). Compassion and caring were to be supreme. Human needs were to be put before animals and rituals. Mankind was to be served and elevated through the institution of the Sabbath, not the other way around. It was clear to Jesus that it was more lawful to do good to people rather than to harm them on the Sabbath—to save a life rather than to take one (Mk. 3:4).

By presenting these truths on the Sabbath and performing so many accompanying miracles, it is not surprising that the people of Jesus' day "were astonished at his doctrine; for his word was with power...And the fame of him went out into every place of the country round about" (Lk. 4:32, 37).

Although its ultimate meaning and fulfillment were found in the days of the Messiah, Jesus Christ, the Sabbath relates to other prophetic time periods as well.

The Scriptures are silent concerning the observance of the Sabbath during the church age. Nine of the Ten Commandments are reiterated in some fashion in the New Testament, but the commandment concerning the Sabbath day is not. The Book of Acts records that Paul and his companions were seen on numerous occasions going into the synagogue on the seventh day of the week; however, this was not out of obligation but, rather, out of practicality. Paul was seeking opportunities to share the gospel of Jesus Christ with those to whom the messianic promises had been made. Further, the early Christians customarily met on the first day of the week—Sunday, the day the Lord Jesus was resurrected—rather than on the seventh day of the week (Acts 20:7).

Following the church age and during the seventieth week of Daniel's prophecy (Dan. 9:27), known as the Tribulation period, observance of the Sabbath may actually become a hindrance to Jewish people who will be fleeing for their lives from the machinations of the Antichrist (Mt. 24:20–21).

The purest form of the Sabbath will be the millennial reign of Jesus Christ on the earth. This period, known in Jewish tradition as the "world to come" or the "Great Sabbath," will be characterized by such perfect rest and harmony that today's Sabbath is considered a mere one-sixtieth of what it will be like during that blissful time.

The New Testament states that the millennial age will be ushered in with the return of Jesus the Messiah. Rabbinical tradition, however, says that instead of waiting passively for the Messiah to come, Jewish people as a whole can initiate their national redemption by keeping the Sabbath. The Talmud states, "If Israel were to keep two Sabbaths according to the [rabbinical] laws thereof, they would be redeemed immediately."[12]

During the Millennium the Sabbath will continue to be observed, with some slight changes in the number of sacrifices offered (Ezek. 46:4). The most likely reason for its observance in that era will be to serve as an ongoing portrait of the rest found in Jesus Christ and His kingdom.

ENDNOTES

[1] Nathan Ausubel. *The Book of Jewish Knowledge* (New York: Crown Publishers, Inc., 1964), 374. Quoting Ahad ha-Am (Asher Ginzberg).

[2] Isodor Grunfeld, *The Sabbath* (New York: Feldheim Publishers, 1954; reprint 1988), 29.

[3] *Ibid.*, p. 32. See also *The Mishnah*, trans. Herbert Danby (New York: Oxford University Press, 1933), Shabbath 7.2.

[4] *Ibid.*, 43, 46.

[5] *The Mishnah*, trans. Herbert Danby (New York: Oxford University Press, 1933), Tamid 7.4.

[6] Joseph H. Hertz, ed., *The Pentateuch and Haftorahs*, 2nd ed. (London: The Soncino Press, 1970), 195.

[7] Joseph H. Hertz, *The Authorised Daily Prayer Book*, rev. ed. (New York: Bloch Publishing Co., 1948), 413.

[8] Ibid., 749.

[9] *The Mishnah*, Shabbath 22.6.

[10] Ibid., 749, Shabbath 15.1.

[11] Hertz, *The Authorised Daily Prayer Book*, 417. Emphasis mine.

[12] *The Babylonian Talmud*, trans. under the editorship of Rabbi Dr. I. Epstein, *et al*, 18 vols. (London: The Soncino Press, 1938), Shabbath 118b.

A table setting for the
Passover Seder

3

PESACH:
PASSOVER AND THE FEAST
OF UNLEAVENED BREAD

*But, as he who hath called you is holy, so be ye
holy in all manner of life, Because it is written, Be
ye holy; for I am holy. . . Forasmuch as ye know
that ye were not redeemed with corruptible things,
like silver and gold, from your vain manner of life
received by tradition from your fathers, But with
the precious blood of Christ, as of a lamb without
blemish and without spot* (1 Pet. 1:15–16, 18–19).

Of all the feasts of Israel, none foreshadows our redemption in
Jesus Christ in such beautiful detail as the festival of
Passover. Congruently, the holy standard of living to which God
calls us is exemplified in the Feast of Unleavened Bread.

Origin and Description of Passover and the Feast of Unleavened Bread

Passover and the Feast of Unleavened Bread are biblical feasts instituted by God and given to the nation of Israel. Their roots are found in the story of the Exodus (Ex. 12:1—13:10). The children of Israel were enslaved in the land of Egypt for 400 years. Then God raised up Moses to lead them out of slavery, into freedom, and toward the promised land. Israel's release from their captors did not come easily, however. Pharaoh's heart was hardened, although the Lord had demonstrated His power over the gods of Egypt through nine plagues. The tenth and last plague broke the will of the stubborn king and served as the historical origin for the Passover holiday.

The enslaved Israelites were instructed by God, through Moses, to select an unblemished male sheep or goat yearling, one to each household, on the tenth day of the month of Nisan. They were to keep it until the 14th day of the month, at which time they were to sacrifice it at twilight. They then took the blood of the lamb and applied it to the doorposts and lintels of their homes. That night, as each household ate the Passover lamb with unleavened bread and bitter herbs, the Lord went through the land of Egypt and struck down the firstborn male of every household and beast. All those whose homes did not have the blood of the Passover lamb applied to the doorposts of their homes were judged. All those who did apply the blood to the doorposts were saved. God said, "the blood shall be to you for a token upon the houses where ye are; and when I see the blood, I will pass over you" (Ex. 12:13).

Since that first Passover night, Jewish people have kept the holiday annually throughout their generations, as God instructed them (Ex. 12:14). But there was only one Passover—only one time when God judged the land of Egypt—only one time when the children of Israel had to apply the blood of the Passover lamb to their homes. All other Passovers since then have been memorials of what occurred on that first Passover. The *holidays* of Passover and Unleavened Bread were therefore established by God for the purpose of remembering (Dt. 16:1, 3). The people of Israel were to remember how God had set them free from the land of slavery.

Although the term *Passover* actually refers to the sacrificial animal, *Passover* is also used in the Bible as a synonym for the Feast of Unleavened Bread (Lk. 22:1). The Feast of Unleavened Bread is one of the three *pilgrim feasts* that all Jewish adult males were commanded to celebrate annually in Jerusalem (Ex. 23:14-15).

Observance of Passover and the Feast of Unleavened Bread

In biblical days the Feast of Unleavened Bread was observed for seven days from the 15th through the 21st of Nisan (March–April) [Lev. 23:6]. Today Israelis and Reform Jews still keep the feast for seven days, while most Jewish people in the Diaspora observe the feast for eight days.

The first and last days of the festival were considered holy days during which, like the Sabbath, no work was to be performed. Only labor necessary for daily sustenance was permitted (Ex. 12:16). Orthodox Jews today apply the work prohibition to the intermediate days of the festival as well.

While the Temple stood, special burnt offerings, grain offerings, and sin offerings were presented to the Lord during the days of Unleavened Bread (Num. 28:17–25). Since the destruction of the Temple in A.D. 70, these offerings have not been included in the holiday's festivities.

Of course, a key element in the observance of the Feast of Unleavened Bread is the bread itself. Bread eaten during the seven festival days could not contain any leavening or fermenting ingredient (Ex. 12:18–20). Furthermore, all *hametz* (food products containing leaven) had to be removed from the home. To accomplish this mandate, specific rituals were developed. The process is called *nullification*.

The procedure for nullification begins even before the festival arrives. It starts with a thorough spring cleaning of the home. Old dishes and cutlery are stored away, and fresh Passover ones take their place. All food products that contain any trace of leaven are discarded. Only goods marked "Kosher for Passover" are purchased. People who have large quantities of leavened products in the home and would suffer significant financial loss by destroying them are permitted to sell them to non-Jewish people and buy them back after the holiday.

The next step in the process of nullification takes place on the evening of the 14th of Nisan. Using the light of one candle, a search for leaven is conducted throughout the house. Any leaven found—which usually includes a few strategically placed crumbs here and there—is swept into a wooden spoon with a feather. The father then recites a prayer nullifying the leaven: "Any leaven and leavening which is in my possession and which I have neither seen, nor destroyed, nor known of, is to be as naught, and as ownerless as the dust of the earth."[1] The next morning, the prayer is repeated as the feather, wooden spoon, and any leaven that turned up during the search are burned, thus ending the process of nullification.

During the days of the Second Temple, Jewish people were instructed by the priests when to have all the hametz removed from their homes and destroyed. The priests would lay two loaves of the thank offering (Lev. 7:13) that were no longer edible on the roof of the Temple portico for everyone to see. When they removed one loaf, the people were no longer permitted to eat anything containing leaven. When they removed the second loaf, it signaled the time for the burning of the hametz, at which time bonfires were lit all around Jerusalem.

It is important that the leaven be removed from the home before midday on the 14th, because in Temple days the Passover sacrifice was slain in late afternoon. Since the paschal sacrifice was not to be offered with leaven (Ex. 34:25), all leaven had to be eliminated during the morning hours.

Nullification may include either a physical destruction of the hametz or a mental renunciation. The Mishnah allows people who are away from home and are not able to return to destroy leaven in their possession to "annul it in his heart."[2]

In Second Temple days, once the leaven had been removed from the premises, it was time to take the chosen Passover lamb to the Temple for sacrifice. (There were so many pilgrims in Jerusalem at Passover [more than two million on one occasion] that the noise of the people and their animals could be heard far away.) Before the holiday commenced, messengers were sent out to the surrounding areas to tell everyone who had flocks and herds to bring them to Jerusalem so that there would be sufficient animals available for the pilgrims to sacrifice and eat.

As people arrived at the Temple Mount with their Passover lambs, which could range in age from eight days to one year old, they awaited the opening of the Temple courtyard doors. The priests then permitted the people to enter the courtyard and divided the crowd into three groups. As the first group entered, the gates were closed behind them and the shofar (ram's horn) was sounded. The stones of the altar and the ramp leading to the altar, as well as the Temple sanctuary itself, had been whitewashed with plaster just for this occasion. The sight of the sparkling clean Temple area must have been magnificent.

The people then killed their animals, and a priest caught the blood of the sacrifice in a basin. Other priests were standing in two lines, those in one line carrying silver basins, and those in the second line carrying gold basins. As the first priest passed the blood-filled basin to the next priest in line, he received an empty basin in return. This exchange continued on down the line until the last priest tossed the blood on the altar, which had a red line around its middle. This line separated sacrificial blood tossed above the line from that tossed below the line, as was the practice at Passover. All of the priests involved in this procedure wore scarlet robes so that, in the event of an accidental spill, the blood on their clothing would not be noticed.

After the sacrifice, the animals were taken by their owners and hung on hooks in the walls and pillars. If all the hooks were in use, men held staves between their shoulders, and the carcasses were hung from the staves. The lambs were then flayed and taken home to be roasted. As the Passover lambs were slain, the Levites sang for each incoming group a collection of psalms called the *Hallel* (Ps. 113—118).

No one was permitted to eat the Passover feast alone. In fact, at least ten individuals had to be identified with each sacrifice, but not all ten had to be present at the Temple when the animal was slain. Non-Jews (Ex. 12:48) and apostate Jews ("foreigner," Ex. 12:43) were not permitted to eat the Passover lamb. They were, however, permitted to eat the unleavened bread and bitter herbs. If people were unable to partake of the Passover because they were unclean or were on a journey, they were permitted to sacrifice the Passover lamb on the 14th of the following month (*Iyyar*) and eat it with unleavened bread and bitter herbs (Num. 9:9–14).

During the evening Passover meal, it was customary to recline on pillows placed on the floor and eat from a low table. Reclining was the symbol of a free person (slaves were required to stand and do the serving), and on this night all were considered free. Today, observant Jews do not recline on the floor but on a pillow placed on the left side, usually in a chair.

During the Passover order of service, called the *seder*, it was obligatory to list and explain the meaning of the three original elements, a custom still observed in modern seders. The meal had to be completed by midnight. A biblical injunction forbade the breaking of any bones of the Passover lamb, even while eating it (Ex. 12:46). Violators of this command were punished with 39 lashes of a whip. Any uneaten portion of the Passover lamb was to be burned on the morning of the 16th of Nisan (unless the 16th fell on a Sabbath, in which case the burning occurred on the morning of the 17th) [Ex. 12:10].

Since the destruction of Jerusalem and the Temple in A.D. 70, the Passover observance has undergone changes. Without a Temple, a priesthood, and a Passover sacrifice, the service has been adapted to the ever-fluctuating condition of the Jewish community. Passover is still a joyful holiday. As preparation is made, the participants anticipate the happy occasion as if they were royalty for a day. The best food is served; the best tableware is used; the best decorations are set out; the best clothing is worn.

On the first night, the synagogue service is held early, so that children may attend. Back in the home, the family comes together to begin the seder. To help remember the events of the Passover, the story is retold with the aid of a booklet called the *Haggadah*, which contains the account of the Passover, various rabbinical commentaries, assorted prayers, and songs. Not every Jewish family reads through the entire Haggadah, because to do so would take hours.

The original Passover was simple. There were only three elements on the table. Since the Exodus, however, other elements have been added, each having its own symbolic meaning.

Wine or Grape Juice: Four times during the Passover seder the cups are filled with wine or grape juice, and a blessing is pronounced. These four cups represent the four ways in which God describes Israel's redemption in Exodus 6:6–7: "I will bring you out from under the burdens of the Egyptians, and I will rid you out of their bondage, and I will redeem you with an outstretched arm, and with great judgments; And I will take you to me for a people." The color of the wine or grape juice is always red, recalling the blood of the Passover lamb.

Elijah's Cup: Based on Malachi 4:5, Jewish tradition teaches that the Prophet Elijah will come one day and announce the arrival of the Messiah. In anticipation of that event, there is an extra place setting and a special cup on the seder table designated just for Elijah. This cup is identified with God's promise in Exodus 6:8: "I will bring you in unto the land," which is interpreted as referring to Israel's final redemption in the last days.

Parsley: This leafy herb is on the table to remember the hyssop used by the Israelites as a brush to apply the blood of the Passover lamb to the doorposts and lintels of their homes (Ex. 12:22).

Salt Water: Salt water is used to symbolize the tears of the Jewish people shed while in bondage.

Charoset: This mixture of chopped apples, nuts, cinnamon, and wine or grape juice represents the bricks and mortar the Israelites made while they were slaves in Egypt.

Hard-boiled Egg: The egg has numerous interpretations. Some view it as a reminder of the festival offering that was sacrificed along with the Passover lamb. Others see it as a symbol of grief over the destruction of the Temple. Some Jewish families eat the egg during the seder, while others simply include it for its symbolic meaning.

Bitter Herbs: Symbolizing the bitter lives of the children of

Israel in Egypt (Ex. 1:14), horseradish is often used for the bitter herbs. Strong horseradish brings tears to the eyes, aiding in the reflection on the bitterness of slavery.

Lettuce: This serves as another form of bitter herbs.

Unleavened Bread: There are three matzo (unleavened bread) crackers on the Passover table. They are often placed inside a special pouch containing three compartments. These three matzos represent the three biblical divisions within the people of Israel. The top piece represents the Cohens (pricsts); the middle piece represents the Levites; the bottom piece represents the Israelites. The matzos serve as a reminder of the unleavened bread the children of Israel ate as they left Egypt in haste (Ex. 12:39).

Roasted Shank Bone of a Lamb: According to the Bible, the holiday of Passover was to be observed only in the city of Jerusalem, site of the Temple, where the Passover lambs were sacrificed for this special occasion (Dt. 16:5–7). Today this is no longer required. Since the destruction of Jerusalem and the Temple in A.D. 70, no Passover lambs have been killed and eaten. Instead, the roasted shank bone of a lamb is placed on the table as a memorial of the Passover sacrifice.

Six of these Passover elements are usually set on a special decorative seder plate, positioned above the matzo pouch.

Once the table is set and all the elements put in place, the evening's festivities begin. The lady of the house greets the holiday with a blessing over the festival candles. After the participants gather at the table, the first cup of wine, the kiddush, is blessed and drunk, following by a hand-washing ceremony. Cleanliness has always been important to the Jewish people. Ceremonial washings played an integral role in biblical Judaism and still do in rabbinical Judaism.

A green vegetable, usually parsley, is then dipped into the salt water and eaten by all of the participants. At this point, the middle matzo is taken from the matzo pouch and broken in half. One half is put back inside the pouch for later use. The other half is wrapped in a cloth and hidden away, to be hunted later by the children. This special piece of unleavened bread is called the *afikomen*.

The story of the Exodus is then recounted, introduced by the youngest child, who poses the question, "Why is this night of Pesach so different from all other nights of the year?" The child then asks four more questions. "On all other nights we may eat either leavened or unleavened bread; why on this night do we eat only unleavened bread? On all other nights we may eat any species of herbs; why on this night do we eat only bitter herbs? On all other nights we do not dip even once; why on this night do we dip twice? On all other nights we eat and drink either sitting or reclining; why on this night do we all recline?"

The answers to these questions form the impetus for explaining the Passover story. Beginning with Abraham's God-given glimpse into Israel's enslaved future (Gen. 15:13-14), the account of Moses and the redemption from Egypt is retold. When the narrative comes to the ten plagues, each participant dips a finger (representing the "finger of God" in judgment) into a goblet and places a drop of wine on the plate as each plague is recited.

As the retelling of the Passover story concludes, two of the Hallel psalms (Ps. 113-114) are spoken, followed by the blessing and drinking of the second cup. All participants then wash their hands, while an appropriate blessing is spoken. A blessing also is pronounced as the upper and middle matzos are broken and distributed for everyone to eat, immediately followed by eating the bitter herbs.

Next a sandwich is formed from the bitter herbs, the charoset, and two pieces of the bottom matzo. Known as a "Hillel sandwich," it originally included meat from the Passover lamb and was instituted by Hillel the Elder, a notable first-century Jewish rabbi, and therefore bears his name.

Finally the time arrives in the service for the festive, often sumptuous holiday meal. Once that is completed, the participants search for and eat the afikomen. This is the moment the children anxiously await. When the previously hidden afikomen is discovered, the fortunate finder brings the enshrouded piece of matzo to the father, who rewards the child, usually with a monetary gift. The afikomen is then broken and distributed for everyone to eat. No other food is eaten after the afikomen has been consumed.

The meal is followed by a prayer of thanksgiving, succeeded by blessing and drinking the third cup of wine. A member of the family is then asked to go to the door, open it, and see if Elijah the prophet is coming.

The remaining Hallel psalms (Ps. 115-118) are then read, followed by blessing and drinking the fourth and final cup. Some observant families then fill Elijah's cup and surround it with all of the other cups, signifying the special place Elijah has in Israel's future redemption.

At the conclusion of the Passover seder, additional festival songs are sung. Looking forward to the coming messianic age, all of the participants cry out with one voice, "Next year in Jerusalem!" With this expression of hope, the first night of the Feast of Unleavened Bread ends.

Of course, beginning with the first evening and continuing throughout the feast, only unleavened bread or matzo is eaten. For years matzo was handmade in a circular shape. When machines began to mass produce unleavened bread, it was shaped in a square to safeguard against leaving behind the corners of cut-out circular matzo and allowing them to ferment, thereby contaminating the whole batch. Matzo has always been baked with puncture holes to permit any trapped air to escape, thus preventing the dough from rising.

The biblical commandment not to eat anything leavened during the Feast of Unleavened Bread was so important that God declared that anyone who disobeyed would be "cut off from Israel" (Ex. 12:15). Being cut off from the congregation of Israel was the worst penalty that could be incurred and was usually reserved for intentional or deliberate offenders. Rabbinical scholars differ as to what being "cut off" actually denoted. It certainly involved death—either premature death in this life or separation from God and His people in the life to come. Because of the severity of the penalty, ultra-Orthodox Jews today eat only matzo that has been "guarded" until the festival (watched continually from the time the grain is cut until the dough is put into the oven to insure that no fermentation has occurred).

Prophecy, Passover, and the Feast of Unleavened Bread

Prophetically, Passover and the Feast of Unleavened Bread relate to both the First and Second Comings of the Messiah, Jesus of Nazareth. The Gospels record that Jesus observed Passover and the Feast of Unleavened Bread on numerous occasions, the most significant being the Passover He celebrated with His disciples on the night He was betrayed. Some customs present in modern seders were also practiced in Jesus' day, but others are new. It is difficult to accurately pinpoint the Passover customs Jesus observed. The Gospel records give only highlights of Jesus' last seder. Similarities between His seder and its modern counterpart are present, to be sure, but are limited.

The Bible relates that two of Jesus' disciples were sent ahead to prepare the Passover (Mk. 14:12–13). It is likely that part of the preparation included confirmation that all leaven had been removed from the house where they were going to keep the festival, as well as assuring that a freshly baked supply of unleavened bread was on hand. Once preparations had been made, Jesus and His disciples partook of His final Passover meal, His Last Supper.

Hand-washing is not mentioned in the Gospel accounts, but at one point during the evening, Jesus got up from supper and washed the disciples' feet (Jn. 13). The object lesson was clear: Not only was Jesus exemplifying the epitome of servanthood, He was also demonstrating a spiritual principle that He had taught many times before. Outward washings are merely symbols of what should be true on the inside; inward, spiritual cleanliness takes precedence over that which is outward. In a parallel passage reiterating this principle, Jesus' disciples were rebuked by the Scribes and the Pharisees for not washing their hands before they ate bread. Jesus' response was pointed and went straight to the heart of the matter: "Hear, and understand: Not that which goeth into the mouth defileth a man, but that which cometh out of the mouth, this defileth a man...those things which proceed out of the mouth come forth from the heart, and they defile the man. For out of the heart proceed evil thoughts, murders, adulteries, fornications, thefts, false witness, blasphemies. These are the things which defile a man; but to eat with unwashed hands defileth not a man" (Mt. 15:10–11, 18–20).

Later that Passover evening, Jesus announced that one of His disciples would betray Him, indicating which one it would be by dipping a sop or morsel of bread and giving it to Judas Iscariot. It is likely that this sop was the "Hillel sandwich" described earlier. Judas, "having received the sop, went immediately out; and it was night" (Jn. 13:30). This was in fulfillment of the messianic prophecy found in Psalm 41:9, "Yea, mine own familiar friend, in whom I trusted, who did eat of my bread, hath lifted up his heel against me."

During His last Passover meal, Jesus partook of the unleavened bread and drank of the Passover cups (Lk. 22:17–20). He and His disciples concluded their Passover seder by singing a hymn (Mt. 26:30). A significant aspect of the Last Supper is that Jesus applied two of the main elements of the seder—the unleavened bread and one of the cups of wine—to Himself.

"When he had given thanks, he broke it [the unleavened bread], and said, Take, eat; this is my body, which is broken for you: this do in remembrance of me" (1 Cor. 11:24). The symbolism was clear. In Jewish teaching, leaven was representative of "the evil impulse of the heart."[3] Jesus Himself applied the allegory to the pervasive, evil doctrine of the Pharisees, Sadducees, and Herod (Mt. 16:11; Mk. 8:15). In applying the symbol of the unleavened bread to His own body, Jesus was saying that His life contained no evil or sin.

"After the same manner also he took the cup, when he had supped, saying, This cup is the new testament in my blood: this do, as often as ye drink it, in remembrance of me" (1 Cor. 11:25). It is important to recognize that in the Passover seder, the third cup immediately follows supper and corresponds with the third promise of Exodus 6:6: "I will redeem you." Thus, the cup of redemption that Jesus took on that last Passover night symbolized what He was about to do through His death. He would shed His blood to bring redemption, the forgiveness of sins. Just as the Passover brought physical redemption, Jesus' death would bring spiritual redemption (Eph. 1:7).

It is because of this symbolism that Christians observe the communion service or partake of the Lord's table. As Passover was established to be a memorial, so too was the communion service. Jesus said, "This do in remembrance of me...For as often as ye eat this bread, and drink this cup, ye do show the Lord's death till he come" (1 Cor. 11:24, 26).

In applying the bread and cup to His own person and ministry, Jesus did far more than just institute a new ordinance to be observed. He clearly stated that the Jewish holidays of Passover and Unleavened Bread pictured or foreshadowed what He, the promised Messiah, would be and do. The three original elements of the Passover tell the story of the redemption found in Jesus Christ.

The Bitter Herbs

Spiritual slavery is much more bitter than mere physical slavery. The Bible teaches that the things we do that are contrary to the will of God—sin—enslave us: "For of whom [or what] a man is overcome, of the same is he brought in bondage" (2 Pet. 2:19). Also, there are "Such as sit in darkness and in the shadow of death, being bound in affliction and iron, Because they rebelled against the words of God, and despised the counsel of the Most High" (Ps. 107:10–11).

Just as the children of Israel were slaves in the land of Egypt, the Bible teaches that we are slaves to sin. Just as they obeyed their taskmasters, so we obey our sin nature. "For the imagination of man's heart is evil from his youth" (Gen. 8:21). Scripture makes it plain that all of mankind is bound in this sinful condition. "The LORD looked down from heaven upon the children of men, to see if there were any that did understand, and seek God. They are all gone aside, they are all together become filthy; there is none that doeth good, no, not one" (Ps. 14:2–3). The resulting penalty is death. "The soul that sinneth, it shall die" (Ezek. 18:20). This involves physical death and spiritual death, or separation from God. "But your iniquities have separated between you and your God, and your sins have hidden his face from you, that he will not hear" (Isa. 59:2).

Since all people are spiritually dead in their trespasses and sins

(Eph. 2:1), it is impossible for them to redeem themselves or others. "None of them can by any means redeem his brother, nor give to God a ransom for him (For the redemption of their soul is precious. . .)" (Ps. 49:7–8). In other words, a sinner cannot pay the spiritual debt of another sinner. Only a sinless person could achieve that. This leads to the second original element in the Passover.

The Unleavened Bread

Leaven in the Scriptures is symbolic of sin. Unleavened bread represents that which has no sin. Only the Messiah is described in the Bible as being without sin—without stain or spot. "He had done no violence, neither was any deceit in his mouth" (Isa. 53:9). As Jesus applied the unleavened bread to His sinless life, His messianic claim became evident. He was the righteous branch of David, the one without violence or deceit. Even His enemies could not rightfully accuse Him of wrongdoing (Jn. 8:46). Jesus knew that because of mankind's sinful condition, spiritual redemption would require someone who was spiritually alive to die on behalf of those who were spiritually dead. He was the only one who could accomplish that, because He was the one who had never sinned. Therefore, although all of mankind has gone astray, God "laid on him the iniquity of us all" (Isa. 53:6). How did He do this? The answer is found in the third original element of the Passover.

The Passover Lamb

On the night of the first Passover, the blood of the Passover lamb had to be applied to the doorposts and lintels of the Israelites' homes, for it was by reason of the blood that God spared those homes from judgment. "When I see the blood, I will pass over you" (Ex. 12:13).

Leviticus 17:11 reveals why the blood was so important: "For the life of the flesh is in the blood; and I have given it to you upon the altar to make an atonement for your souls; for it is the blood that maketh an atonement for the soul." The shedding of blood—the substitution of one life for another—brought atonement for sins. In the same way, the Messiah redeemed all of mankind from the bondage of sin by shedding His blood and giving up His life so that we might live (Isa. 53:5).

All of this was typified in the Passover lamb, whose antitype was Jesus of Nazareth. Just as the Passover lamb was to be without blemish, so Jesus was without stain, blemish, or sin. "Forasmuch as ye know that ye were not redeemed with corruptible things...But with the precious blood of Christ, as of a lamb without blemish and without spot" (1 Pet. 1:18–19). Just as the Passover lamb was to die without any of its bones being broken, so Jesus died without any of His bones being broken, which was unusual for death by crucifixion (Jn. 19:36). Just as the Passover lamb was not to be sacrificed at any place but Jerusalem, so Jesus was sacrificed at Jerusalem. Finally, just as the Passover lamb died as a substitute, so Jesus died in our place as our substitute (Rom. 5:8).

As a reminder of the Passover lamb today, Jewish people place a lifeless shank bone on the seder table, for since the Temple was destroyed in A.D. 70, there have been no sacrifices. But this is in accordance with Scripture, because now there is no need for sacrifice. The Scriptures state, "But this man [Jesus], after he had offered one sacrifice for sins forever, sat down on the right hand of God" (Heb. 10:12), indicating, just as He said, "It is finished [or completed]" (Jn. 19:30).

For centuries Jewish people have longed for and anticipated the coming of the Messiah. It was believed among the ancient sages that because Israel's first redemption occurred on Nisan 15, so too on that date the Messiah would reveal Himself and usher in Israel's future redemption. It is of no small significance, then, that Jesus of Nazareth chose to apply the messianic connotations of the Passover to Himself on the first night of Unleavened Bread, which would, of course, have been Nisan 15.

As we have already seen, Elijah plays an important role in the observance of Passover. His duty is to herald the arrival of the Messiah, who, as noted earlier, is expected to come at Passover. This, in fact, was the mission of John the Baptizer, who came "in the spirit and power of Elijah" (Lk. 1:17). Jesus Himself said of John, "I say unto you, That Elijah is come already, and they knew him not" (Mt. 17:12). In accordance with prophecy, therefore, Elijah, in the person of John the Baptizer, did come and announce the coming of the Messiah with the proclamation, "Behold the Lamb of God, who taketh away the sin of the world" (Jn. 1:29).

Thus, through the three original Passover elements and other related prophecies, God's tremendous plan of spiritual redemption is revealed. And, in the person of Jesus Christ, it is all fulfilled. "Christ, our passover, is sacrificed for us" (1 Cor. 5:7).

Concerning the future of the holidays of Passover and Unleavened Bread, it is important to note that on the night of the Last Supper, Jesus announced that He would not eat the Passover again "until it be fulfilled in the kingdom of God" (Lk. 22:16). Jesus knew that before the kingdom could come, the redemptive meaning of the Passover had to be fulfilled, and He accomplished that through His death.

Following His resurrection, He ascended on high where He sits at the right hand of God, ministering as our High Priest. One day He will come back to the earth to set up His kingdom and restore the glory of Israel. At that time, when Jesus' Millennial Kingdom has been established, the Passover and the Feast of Unleavened Bread will again be observed (Ezek. 45:21-24), perhaps as a memorial of the finished work of Christ and, as with the redemption from Egypt, as a memorial of Israel's redemption from the nations (Jer. 16:14-15).

ENDNOTES

[1] Rabbi Meyer Berlin, *et al*, eds., *Encyclopedia Talmudica*, 3 vols. (Jerusalem: Talmudic Encyclopedia Institute, 1978), vol. 3, 586-587.

[2] *The Mishnah*, trans. Herbert Danby (New York: Oxford University Press, 1933), Pesahim 3.7.

[3] *The Babylonian Talmud*, trans. under the editorship of Rabbi Dr. I. Epstein, *et al*, 18 vols. (London: The Soncino Press, 1938), Berachot 17a.

בִּימֵי שְׁפֹט הַשֹּׁפְטִים וַיְהִי רָעָב בָּאָרֶץ וַיֵּלֶךְ
אִישׁ מִבֵּית לֶחֶם יְהוּדָה לָגוּר בִּשְׂדֵי מוֹאָב הוּא
וְאִשְׁתּוֹ וּשְׁנֵי בָנָיו: וְשֵׁם הָאִישׁ אֱלִימֶלֶךְ וְשֵׁם אִשְׁתּוֹ נָעֳמִי וְשֵׁם
שְׁנֵי בָנָיו מַחְלוֹן וְכִלְיוֹן אֶפְרָתִים מִבֵּית לֶחֶם יְהוּדָה וַיָּבֹאוּ שְׂדֵי
מוֹאָב וַיִּהְיוּ שָׁם: וַיָּמָת אֱלִימֶלֶךְ אִישׁ נָעֳמִי וַתִּשָּׁאֵר הִיא וּשְׁנֵי
בָנֶיהָ: וַיִּשְׂאוּ לָהֶם נָשִׁים מֹאֲבִיּוֹת שֵׁם הָאַחַת עָרְפָּה וְשֵׁם הַשֵּׁנִית

Shavuot, the Feast of Weeks—
The Harvest according to
the Book of Ruth

4

SHAVUOT:
THE FEAST OF WEEKS

The world's longest wall stands in northern China. Roughly following the border of Mongolia, the wall stretches more than 1,500 miles. For most of its length, it is 25 feet high and 12 feet across, wide enough for horses to travel upon. Taking almost 1,500 years to complete, its purpose was to keep invaders out and protect those within. Today the Great Wall of China stands as one of the most renowned marvels of the world, an ancient monument to fear, isolationism, and separatism.

The Bible speaks of another wall, not tangible but present nevertheless. It is not made of brick and mortar but of "the law of commandments contained in ordinances" (Eph. 2:15). Referred to as "the middle wall of partition" (Eph. 2:14), it is a wall that, in effect, has brought about the same consequences as the Great Wall of China. The resulting isolation and separation are between Jews and Gentiles. As one writer put it, "The post-exilic history of Judaism became the history of a 'fenced' community. But a

fence while it preserves, also excludes. The Torah, which differ-
entiated the Jew from others, also separated him from them."[1]

Despite the existence of this "middle wall of partition," God
ordained that one day it would fall like the walls of Jericho. How
would God accomplish this? The story is foreshadowed and told
through one of Israel's most neglected festivals, Shavuot or the
Feast of Weeks.

Origin and Description of Shavuot

Shavuot (lit., *weeks*) is another of the holy convocations
ordained by God and given to the nation of Israel. Shavuot was
the second of the three pilgrim festivals that all adult Jewish
males were required to attend at Jerusalem.

The Feast of Weeks (Ex. 34:22) is also known in Scripture by
other names. It is referred to as the "feast of harvest" (Ex. 23:16)
because it inaugurated the beginning of the wheat harvest. It is
called the "day of the first fruits" (Num. 28:26) because its primary purpose was to bring a designated portion of the harvest, the
"first fruits," into the Temple as an act of dedication to God in
recognition of His provision. The festival is also termed in the
New Testament as "Pentecost" (lit., *fiftieth*) [Acts 2:1], signifying
the *fiftieth* day from the waving of the *omer* (*sheaf*) of first fruits
(Lev. 23:15–16).

Some have separated the act of waving the omer from the Feast
of Shavuot and called it a holiday in its own right, the Feast of
First Fruits. Although the Christologicals' reasons for doing so
are understandable, there is no textual support for such a separation. Both the so-called Feast of First Fruits and the Feast of
Weeks are inextricably linked. While only the latter is designated as a day of "holy convocation," together they serve as the
bookends of one central theme—first fruits. Waving the omer
denoted the first fruits of the barley harvest, and waving the two

loaves on Pentecost denoted the first fruits of the wheat harvest. Furthermore, these two occasions were divinely bound together by the injunction to count a certain number of days from the first event to the second because Shavuot is not given a fixed date of observance in the Scriptures. It is impossible to know when to observe the Feast of Weeks without taking into account the waving of the omer. You cannot keep the second without keeping the first. Thus, for the sake of this discussion, the Feast of First Fruits and the Feast of Weeks will be examined collectively, as part of the same topic, and together will be labeled Shavuot or Pentecost.

In rabbinical writings, the holiday of Shavuot was dubbed *Atzeret* (*solemn assembly*). Just as the Feast of Tabernacles has an extra day of observance—a day of solemn assembly (Lev. 23:36)—likewise the rabbis considered Shavuot to be an extra day or an extension of the Feast of Passover.

Shavuot has also been termed by the rabbis as the Festival of Revelation because it is principally an agricultural holiday and has no memorial significance. Apart from remembering what it was like to be a slave in Egypt (Dt. 16:12), Shavuot does not look back to any historical event related to the nation of Israel, as do the holidays of Passover and Tabernacles. Because they feared that the festival would lose all religious meaning and importance, especially among Jews in the Diaspora, the rabbis chose to tie Shavuot to a meaningful episode in Israel's history.

The episode they chose was the giving of the Law at Mount Sinai. Exodus 19:1 states that the Israelites arrived at Mount Sinai on the first day of the third month, Sivan. According to rabbinical calculations, God spoke to the people of Israel on the sixth day of the month, the traditional day on which Shavuot is observed. Although it is possible that the two events coincided on the calendar, the Bible does not state or even intimate that the Law was given at Sinai on the traditional date of Shavuot. Even if it did, when God outlined the purpose and practice of the holiday in Leviticus 23 and other passages, He did not indicate that it was associated with the events at Mount Sinai.

Nevertheless, by about at least the second century A.D., the festival of Pentecost or Revelation became known as the day on which God gave the Torah (law or instruction) to the people of Israel. Jewish tradition states that God offered the Torah to all the nations of the world, but only one nation would accept its stringent demands—Israel. Along with the written Torah, it is taught that God also gave the oral Torah to Moses on Mount Sinai. The oral Torah is composed of all the rabbinical commentaries on the Old Testament that were passed down orally from generation to generation and eventually put into writing. Together they make up the Talmud and other authoritative works.

The importance of the giving of the Law, both written and oral, to the nation of Israel cannot be overemphasized. It is seen not only as the ultimate goal of the redemption at Passover, but is also looked upon as the protecting, binding force of Jewish identity throughout the centuries. As one Jewish writer stated, "Torah is the essence of our unique faith and lifestyle, the material which must be transmitted from generation to generation if we are to remain an eternal nation. Torah is the historical gene which unites the generations."[2]

Observance of Shavuot

Unlike some of the other festivals, there are only a few precepts assigned to Shavuot, and they center around the presentation of the first fruits to God.

The Shavuot season began with the waving of the omer. God prescribed that once the children of Israel entered the promised land and reaped a harvest, they were to "bring a sheaf of the first fruits of [their] harvest unto the priest, And he [would] wave the sheaf before the LORD" (Lev. 23:10–11).

This speaks of the harvest of the barley crop. The omer was to be the first and best of the year's produce. Although, according to rabbinical rules, the omer could be gathered from anywhere within the land of Israel, it was usually taken from the area near the Temple in Jerusalem, especially since the tribe of Judah was known for its high-quality barley.

When it was time to reap the omer, a delegation from the Temple went into the fields, where bunches of barley, previously tied together for easier reaping, waited. Since reaping the omer was considered a momentous event, large crowds from neighboring towns gathered to watch. The reaping was so important that it could be done even on the Sabbath. The reaping was performed by three Temple officials, each having his own sickle and basket. After sunset (the beginning of a new day on the Jewish calendar), the officials asked three questions, three times each: "Is the sun set? Is this a sickle? Is this a basket?" The crowd looking on responded to each question with a resounding "Yes!"

Once the barley first fruits were cut and put into the baskets, the officials carried it back to the Temple area, where it was dried, beaten, and thoroughly sifted into fine flour. Some accounts indicate that it was sifted as many as 13 times. Based on Leviticus 2:11, all meal or grain offerings were to be unleavened. Because the omer was considered a meal offering, it was unleavened. As with other meal offerings, oil and frankincense were added to the omer (Lev. 2:1).

The omer was waved during the early daylight hours. The priest took one-tenth of the omer flour and brought it to the bronze altar. He then climbed the ramp and stood on the east side of the altar, where he waved the omer before the Lord, swinging the container of sifted flour forward, backward, up, and down. He then went to the west side of the altar, took a handful of the flour, and threw it into the fire. The remainder of the omer meal was then given to the priests for their personal consumption. Various sacrifices, meal offerings, and drink offerings accompanied the waving of the omer (Lev. 23:12–13).

After the omer was waved before the Lord, everyone in Jerusalem was permitted to buy, sell, and eat the new produce from the harvest. Those outside the city limits of Jerusalem had to wait until midday to use the new crops, to insure that the omer had been waved before they partook of the harvest.

During Temple days, a debate took place over which day the omer was to be waved. The issue was important because it not only affected the ritual of the omer, but also the date of Shavuot 50 days later. The biblical text states that the omer was to be brought on "the next day after the sabbath" (Lev. 23:11, 15). The dispute concerned the interpretation of the word *sabbath*. If it referred to the weekly Sabbath (Friday night to Saturday night) during the seven days of the Feast of Unleavened Bread, the omer was waved on Sunday. But if the text referred to the first day of the Feast of Unleavened Bread, which was also a Sabbath day, the day for waving the omer would be variable, depending on which day of the week the first day of Unleavened Bread fell. The Sadducees held to the first option; the Pharisees took the second. After much wrangling, the Pharisaic position prevailed. Therefore, the date for waving the omer and beginning to count the days to Shavuot was established as Nisan 16, the day following the first day (and Sabbath) of the Feast of Unleavened Bread. This day was accepted in Second Temple days and is still followed today.

Once the omer was reaped, they began to count the days to the Feast of Shavuot. The Bible says it started at the time when the sickle was first put to the grain (Dt. 16:9) and lasted for seven weeks or 49 days, the 50th day being Shavuot (Lev. 23:15–16).

Today this numbering process is known as the Counting of the Omer. It takes place in the evening of Nisan 16, the second night of the Feast of Unleavened Bread. As soon as the stars come out, the counting is done aloud by all adult Jewish males, who state both the number of days and the number of weeks that have progressed to that point. For example, on the 12th day they say, "Today is the 12th day, making one week and five days of the omer." This procedure is repeated every evening for 49 days. They do not count on the 50th day because that is Shavuot itself.

The counting of the omer is also a prolonged period of partial mourning. For 32 days no weddings are performed, no music is enjoyed, and no hair is cut. This custom, believed to have started around A.D. 500, is said to commemorate various Jewish tragedies that took place during the counting of the omer. In particular, one famous rabbi, Akiva (ca. A.D. 135), is said to have lost approximately 24,000 students to a plague, which ended on the 33rd day of the counting. To celebrate the end of the plague, a semi-holiday was established, known as *Lag Ba-Omer* (lit., *33rd of Omer*). On this day the mourning ceases, weddings are held, music is enjoyed, and hair is cut. In Israel, schools are closed.

In Temple days, as the counting of the omer reached its climax and the Feast of Shavuot drew near, excitement and preparations intensified. Because Pentecost is also the day of the first fruits, worshipers busily prepared for the pilgrimage to Jerusalem with their first fruit offerings. Earlier, the pilgrims tied the first ripe fruits of their harvests with rope or string. Sometimes zealous worshipers designated whole fields of crops as their first fruits offering. No matter the amount, according to rabbinical guidelines, the fruits had to originate within the land of Israel. Jews living outside the land in the Diaspora apparently were expected to attend the feast but were not obligated to bring a first fruit offering.

Seven kinds of first fruits were accepted for the festival: "Wheat, and barley, and vines, and fig trees, and pomegranates...olive oil, and honey" (Dt. 8:8). Wheat was the foremost offering because Pentecost occurred at the time of the beginning of the wheat harvest. People living near Jerusalem brought fresh fruit as an offering. Those from far away brought dried fruit. None of these first fruits could be presented to the Lord prior to Pentecost (except, of course, for barley at the waving of the omer). The seven kinds of fruit could be brought in either seven different baskets or, as was most probably the case, in one basket with each species separated by some type of covering, the barley being on the bottom and the grapes on the top. The baskets were adorned with live pigeons to be used for burnt offerings at the festival. The wealthy brought their fruits in baskets covered with silver and gold, while those less privileged brought their offerings in wicker baskets of peeled willow branches.

Tens of thousands of people made their way to Jerusalem for the festival, coming from near and far and from all points of the compass. The second chapter of the Book of Acts lists 15 different regions from which Jewish worshipers came for the Feast of Pentecost. They came en masse, occasionally the entire membership of a synagogue or whole districts together. So many people came up to Jerusalem for the Feast of Pentecost and the other two pilgrim festivals that they often became occasions for large demonstrations against Roman rule. On one occasion, just a few short years after the birth of Jesus, thousands of Jewish worshipers gathered in Jerusalem for the Feast of Pentecost. While there, an insurrection arose against a corrupt Roman official named Sabinus. Thousands of Jews lost their lives in the conflict, many being crucified. Whenever a pilgrim holiday of the Jews arrived, the Roman soldiers stationed in Jerusalem went into a heightened state of alert, ready for any uprising or riot.

As they traveled onward, the holiday pilgrims journeyed up to Jerusalem. During the day they sang songs of praise to God and rejoiced in His goodness. At night they slept in the squares of the towns through which they passed. Preceding their procession was an ox, its horns covered in gold and its head adorned with a wreath of olive leaves. A flute player also preceded the group, playing his instrument all the way into the city of Jerusalem. Once near their destination, the excited pilgrims sent word ahead of their imminent arrival. The chief priests and officers of the Temple came out to greet them, and people in the city gave the travelers a hearty welcome as they entered and made their way to the Temple Mount.

Arriving at the Temple area, the holiday worshipers put their baskets on their shoulders and carried their first fruits into the Temple Court. Even King Agrippa II, whom Paul declared to be an "expert in all customs and questions which are among the Jews" (Acts 26:3), participated in this act. As the pilgrims entered the Temple Court, the Levites sang Psalm 30:1: "I will extol thee, O LORD; for thou hast lifted me up, and hast not made my foes to rejoice over me."

With their baskets on their shoulders, the worshipers then repeated after the priests the declaration of Deuteronomy 26:3: "I profess this day unto the LORD thy God, that I am come unto the country which the LORD swore unto our fathers to give us." They then took the baskets off their shoulders and held them at the top as the priests held them underneath. Together the priests and worshipers waved the first fruits before the Lord, forward and backward, up and down. The worshipers again repeated after the priests a portion of Scripture (this time Dt. 26:5–10), left their baskets of first fruits next to the altar, bowed down in worship to God, and departed. The priests could then consume the first fruits, but they had to be sure they were in a state of ritual cleanliness. If they ate the first fruits while unclean, they were subject to the death penalty.

On the day of Shavuot the waving and offering of the two loaves also took place, as the Lord prescribed in Leviticus 23:16-17: "and ye shall offer a new meal offering unto the LORD. Ye shall bring out of your habitations two wave loaves of two tenth parts; they shall be of fine flour; they shall be baked with leaven; they are the first fruits unto the LORD."

Because it was unlawful to bake the two loaves on the actual day of Shavuot, it being a Sabbath day, they were baked the day before. The procedure started by taking fresh wheat grain, which was then turned into fine flour by sifting it 12 times. Two measures of this fine flour were used to make the two loaves. Unlike most other meal or grain offerings, God instructed that the two loaves be baked with leaven. They were kneaded and rolled separately in the city of Jerusalem and then brought to the Temple Court, where they were baked separately. Each loaf was approximately two feet long and one foot wide. Each loaf had *horns*, each one about three inches high, placed similarly to the four horns on the bronze altar. At the moment the two loaves crusted in the oven, they were dedicated to God.

During the daylight hours of Pentecost, the two loaves were presented to God. Unlike most other meal offerings, they were not offered with oil and frankincense (Lev. 2:1). When the two loaves were ready to be waved, they were brought to the bronze altar. The priest stood at the top of the altar on the east side and put his hands under the two loaves, as well as two lambs for a peace offering (Lev. 23:20). He then swung them before the Lord, forward, backward, up, and down. Unlike the omer, none of the two loaves was thrown into the fire. Instead, the full two loaves were given to the priests for their consumption. Other biblical requirements for this day included refraining from work

(Lev. 23:21) and rejoicing (Dt. 16:11).

Today the holiday of Shavuot has changed dramatically. First, it is practiced by very few in the Jewish community other than the Orthodox. Second, because there is no Temple in Jerusalem, the ceremonies of the omer, first fruits, and two loaves are no longer performed. Third, the emphasis of the holiday has shifted from first fruits to the tradition of the giving of the Torah at Mount Sinai. For example, entertaining a rabbinical Torah scholar in the home is seen as the equivalent of offering first fruits. Also, a custom was instituted in the Middle Ages to introduce young children to the study of the Torah. On Shavuot, Bible verses were written on a small tablet. Honey was poured over the writing, and the children licked it off the tablet. Other treats were also distributed to impress upon the children that studying the Torah was sweet (Ps. 19:10). Some observant Jews still practice this custom.

The Feast of Shavuot is observed for two days, the sixth and seventh of Sivan (May-June). Reform Jews and Jews in Israel observe it for only one day. Readings and prayers in the synagogue include the Book of Ruth, because its story took place around harvest time and because Ruth is seen as a good example of a person who was willing to take upon herself the yoke of the Torah. In memory of King David, a descendant of Ruth, the entire Book of Psalms is also read, along with Exodus 19 and 20. When the Ten Commandments are read, the congregants rise from their seats out of respect.

Many Reform congregations, along with some Conservative, choose to hold confirmation ceremonies for their young people on Shavuot, symbolizing the charge and commitment of the young people to observe the Torah in like manner as the children of Israel did at Mount Sinai. Other customs associated with Shavuot include decorating the home and synagogue with greenery and sometimes putting roses on the Torah scrolls. It also is customary to eat cheesecake, blintzes (cheese crepes), *kreplach* (triangular dumplings filled with meat or cheese), and two loaves of holiday bread, reminiscent of the two loaves eaten in the Temple.

Prophecy and Shavuot

Prophetically, the holiday of Shavuot, with its theme of first fruits, carries with it numerous applications or fulfillments. Generally, the Bible applies the concept of first fruits to the people of God. Like first fruits, the people of God are chosen, designated, choice, and special.

Specifically, Israel is referred to in Scripture as God's first fruits. "Israel was holiness unto the LORD, and the first fruits of his increase; all that devour him shall offend; evil shall come upon them, saith the LORD" (Jer. 2:3). Just as people were not to eat the first fruits of the new harvest because they were holy to the Lord, so too Israel is holy to the Lord and is not to be attacked or devoured. Those who did eat of the first fruits (apart from the ritually cleansed priests) were punished (Lev. 22:10–16). Likewise, those who harm God's ancient people Israel will also be punished (Gen. 12:3).

Believers in the church age, both individually (1 Cor. 16:15) and collectively (Jas. 1:18), are also called first fruits. Finally, the 144,000 from the tribes of Israel who will be sealed during the Tribulation period (Rev. 7:4) are described as first fruits (Rev. 14:4).

Most importantly, the prophetic theme of first fruits is applied in the New Testament to the person and work of Jesus of Nazareth, the Messiah. In Him, the ultimate meaning and purpose for the ritual of first fruits is explained and fulfilled. The Apostle Paul said of Jesus, "But now is Christ risen from the dead and become the first fruits of them that slept. For since by man came death, by man came also the resurrection of the dead. For as in Adam all die, even so in Christ shall all be made alive; But every man in his own order: Christ the first fruits; afterward they that are Christ's at his coming" (1 Cor. 15:20–23).

In context, Paul cleared up a question that was troubling the Corinthian believers. The problem was whether or not there really is a resurrection of the dead (1 Cor. 15:12). Paul answered that the dead most definitely will be resurrected. To prove his point, Paul pointed to the resurrection of Jesus Christ. If the Messiah has not been resurrected, contrary to what had been proclaimed, no one else will be resurrected (1 Cor. 15:14-18). But Jesus was raised from the dead, and therefore those who believe in Him will likewise be raised from the dead.

God raised Jesus from the dead, not just physically, but spiritually (1 Pet. 3:18). Jesus was made alive in spirit and body. He became the first fruits of those who would be resurrected, not only in their bodies but also in their spirits, as they placed their faith in Him (Col. 2:13). This is the underlying theme of the Feast of Shavuot, the Day of First Fruits. Beginning with waving the omer and climaxing with waving the two loaves, offering the first fruits represents new life, resurrection, and life from the dead.

The omer typifies the resurrection of Jesus. It was an unleavened meal offering. In Scripture, leaven is symbolic of sin; thus, an unleavened offering represents that which has no sin. Just as the omer was unleavened, so Jesus the Messiah was without sin and was therefore raised from the dead, "according to the spirit of holiness" (Rom. 1:4).

As with most meal offerings, the omer was mixed with oil and frankincense. The only meal offerings that did not have oil and frankincense were those associated with sin (Lev. 5:11). In the Bible, oil is symbolic of the Holy Spirit, and frankincense is symbolic of communion with God through prayer. In the resurrection of Jesus Christ, we see both the working of the Holy Spirit (Rom.

8:11) and communion with God the Father through prayer (Heb. 5:7). The presence of these two elements in the offering and resurrection of Jesus Christ further attests to His sinless life.

The omer also typifies the resurrection of Jesus in the timing of its presentation to the Lord. As seen earlier, the Pharisees believed that the omer should be waved before the Lord on the 16th day of Nisan, the second day of Passover, regardless of the day of the week. The Sadducees also believed that the omer should be waved during the Passover week, but only on Sunday. The correct view is debatable, but the indisputable fact is that Jesus died at the beginning of Passover week and was resurrected on Sunday during Passover week, fulfilling the types of both the Passover lamb and the omer first fruits.

As the omer typifies the resurrection of Jesus Christ, the two loaves as first fruits typify the birth of the church. The word *church* literally means *called out ones*. In the New Testament it primarily refers to that group of people, whether Jewish or Gentile, who have experienced a spiritual regeneration, or new birth as a result of placing their faith in Jesus as their Messiah and Savior. At the very moment of their new birth, they are united with Him through the baptism of the Holy Spirit (1 Cor. 12:13). Together these believers in Christ constitute an assembly of people called out to form a spiritual union, known in Scripture as the *body of Christ*, with Jesus as the "head" (Eph. 1:22–23).

When the Bible speaks of the church, it is not referring to a building, a place of worship, or a denomination. Church buildings are merely places where local, smaller manifestations of the larger, universal assembly of believers meet for worship. The church is not made of brick and mortar; it is made of people who have been redeemed by the blood of Christ and have been united in Him through His Spirit.

This union began on the day of Pentecost, the day when the

two loaves—the first fruits—were waved before the Lord. Along with the followers of Jesus, devout Jews "out of every nation under heaven" (Acts 2:5) had gathered at Jerusalem. They were the pilgrims who had come to celebrate the holiday of Shavuot. "And when the day of Pentecost was fully come, they were all with one accord in one place. And suddenly there came a sound from heaven like a rushing mighty wind, and it filled all the house where they were sitting. And there appeared unto them cloven tongues as of fire, and it sat upon each of them. And they were all filled with the Holy Spirit, and began to speak with other tongues, as the Spirit gave them utterance...Now when this was noised abroad, the multitude came together, and were confounded, because every man heard them speak in his own language" (Acts 2:1–4, 6).

On the day of Pentecost, God performed a miracle as a sign or indication that He was doing something new. Followers of Jesus were given the ability to speak in other languages so that they could proclaim the good news of the Messiah to Jews from all nations. This proclamation of God's Word in foreign languages was not only a fulfillment of prophecy (1 Cor. 14:21–22), it was an event that especially grabbed the attention of Jewish worshipers on Shavuot. According to Jewish tradition, when God gave the Torah at Mount Sinai on the day of Pentecost, He did so speaking in all the languages of the world—70 in number. Hearing Jesus' followers miraculously speak in other languages, particularly on the day of Pentecost, naturally caught the ear of observant Jews familiar with that legend.

The preaching of God's Word on Pentecost resulted in the spiritual resurrection of three thousand souls (Acts 2:41). It also revealed a secret that had not been disclosed before that day: God planned to establish a new entity called the church, wherein Jews and Gentiles could have equal access to God with no distinctions between them. "For there is no difference between the Jew and the Greek; for the same Lord over all is rich unto all that call upon him" (Rom. 10:12; cp. Eph. 3:1–6).

The story of Ruth, read in the synagogues on Shavuot, is a beautiful picture of the way in which God invites both Jews and Gentiles to come to Him through the Messiah. Jesus Himself said, "I am the good shepherd...and I lay down my life for the sheep. And other sheep I have, that are not of this fold; them also I must bring, and they shall hear my voice; and there shall be one fold, and one shepherd" (Jn. 10:14–16).

Even though two loaves were waved before the Lord on the day of Pentecost, they were considered one offering. They were presented in a state of unity, their particles having been baked and joined together to form a new whole. In the same way, the church is composed of two separate groups of people—Jews and Gentiles—joined together to make one new entity. "But now in Christ Jesus ye [Gentiles] who once were far off are made near by the blood of Christ. For he is our peace, who hath made both [Jews and Gentiles] one, and hath broken down the middle wall of partition between us, Having abolished in his flesh the enmity, even the law of commandments contained in ordinances, to make in himself of two one new man, so making peace; And that he might reconcile both [Jews and Gentiles] unto God in one body by the cross, having slain the enmity thereby, And came and preached peace to you [Gentiles] who were afar off, and to them [Jews] that were near. For through him we both [Jews and Gentiles] have access by one Spirit unto the Father" (Eph. 2:13–18).

The Berlin Wall separated East Germany from West Germany for years, but when it came down, the two countries became one. In the same way, but in a much greater sense, the wall of division separating Jews and Gentiles has been torn down through the work of Jesus Christ, enabling God to forge the two groups into one body (Gal. 3:28).

This does not mean that the church is perfect. On the contrary, just as the two loaves on Shavuot were baked with leaven, symbolic of the presence of sin, so too the church contains leaven or sin from which it will not be completely purified until Jesus returns. Those who would discredit the whole body of Christ because of the failures of a few would do well to remember that the church is not made up of perfect saints; it is made up of sinners saved by the grace of God.

There are two other prophetic aspects of the Feast of Shavuot. The first deals with the time between Pentecost and the holiday that follows it on the Jewish calendar, the Feast of Trumpets or Rosh Hashanah. There are almost four months between the two, longer than any other span separating major biblical festivals. The prophetic implication is that this elongated interval pictures the period of time in which we now live, known as the church age, which is seen as a parenthesis in God's program for the nation of Israel.

The remaining prophetic aspect of the Feast of Shavuot deals with its place in the future Millennial Kingdom of Jesus the Messiah. The Scriptures do not specify that Shavuot will be observed during that period, although it may be included in those feasts mentioned in Ezekiel 45:17. There also is a reference to bringing first fruits at that time (Ezek. 44:30).

ENDNOTES

[1] W. D. Davis, *Paul and Rabbinic Judaism: Some Rabbinic Elements in Pauline Theology* (New York: Harper & Row Publishers, 1948), 62.
[2] Rabbi Shlomo Riskin, "Timeless Message: Dealing with Present by Understanding the Past," *JUF News*, May 1993, 51.

Sounding the Shofar on Rosh Hashanah

5

ROSH HASHANAH:
THE JEWISH NEW YEAR

A s darkness fell, a small Jewish family began walking to the synagogue. They were alone. Then little bands of families and friends slowly appeared from between trees, from neighboring houses, and from dimly lit side streets. Soon they became a silent stream of holiday penitents, all converging on the local *shul* (synagogue). Some of the worshipers' heads were covered; others were not. Some carried prayer books; some were empty-handed.

As the service began, hundreds found their way to their seats. Holiday greetings were exchanged, even as the *cantor* opened with the festival chants. The buzz of continuing conversations eventually led the rabbi to tap on the pulpit microphone for attention.

To an impartial observer, the demeanor of most of the people in the congregation might have been interpreted as indifferent or even apathetic. Over there a man and his wife were kibitzing (joking) with friends. A few rows ahead young college men were scanning the crowd for young ladies. Nearby a small boy was enjoying a game of leaning his head back on his chair, causing his *yarmulke* (skullcap) to fall off. In a neighboring seat a woman was sitting with her head propped up on her arm, her eyes closed. All the while, the cantor chanted, the a cappella choir sang, and the rabbi announced the page numbers in the prayer book. Attention became somewhat more focused when the rabbi delivered his sermon. But the restless congregants had heard the theme innumerable times before and looked on seemingly uninterested.

Soon it was all over. The worshipers were on their feet, kissing loved ones, saying *"Gut Yontev"* (*Good Holiday*) or "Happy New Year." The crowd walked home as quietly as it had come, silently disappearing between the trees, into neighboring houses, and down dimly lit side streets.

The experience of this single synagogue is not uncommon to the majority of American Jews. Although they may not attend the synagogue at any other time of the year, on this particular day—as well as ten days later—most people in the Jewish community attempt to attend the services. It is the holiest time on the Jewish calendar. It is the holiday of Rosh Hashanah, the Jewish New Year.

Origin and Description of Rosh Hashanah

The festival of Rosh Hashanah was instituted by God and given to the nation of Israel (Num. 29:1–6). Together with Yom Kippur, Rosh Hashanah is part of the high holidays of Judaism. Both Rosh Hashanah and Yom Kippur are referred to as the "Days of Awe" because during this time an individual's fate is inscribed (on Rosh Hashanah) and sealed (on Yom Kippur) for the coming year. The ten days from Rosh Hashanah to Yom Kippur inclusively are considered "Ten Days of Penitence," during which people are admonished to repent of their sins and perform good deeds in order to merit an inscription in the Book of Life.

On the Jewish calendar, Rosh Hashanah opens the New Year. However, there are actually four Jewish New Year's Days. Nisan 1 begins the religious New Year. Elul 1 was used in ancient times to determine the tithing of animals. Shevat 15 was used to determine the tithing of fruit. Tishri 1, Rosh Hashanah, starts the civil New Year.

Rosh Hashanah (meaning *Head* or *Beginning of the Year*) is also known by three other names: The Day of Judgment, the Day of the Sounding of the Shofar (ram's horn), and the Day of Remembrance. Although not taught in Scripture, it is believed that on Rosh Hashanah God sits in judgment of the whole universe. Like sheep passing before a shepherd, who decides which ones will live and which ones will be slaughtered, on this Day of Judgment God evaluates the merits of people and nations. He rules which nations will have plenty and which will lack; which will have war and which will know peace. He decrees which individuals will have good fortune and which will suffer calamity; which will prosper and which will experience poverty and want; which will live for another year and which will die. This theme of God's judgment is emphasized more than any other on Rosh Hashanah.

The judgment on Rosh Hashanah does not decide a person's eternal destiny. Rosh Hashanah is for judgment concerning earthly matters. The judgment handed down on that day, with its subsequent recording in the Book of Life, decides a person's fate in this life for the coming year. That is not to say that people's actions do not impact the final judgment of their souls after they die, but on Rosh Hashanah their behavior is judged only for the here and now and not for the hereafter.

The verdict is settled by opening three books: one listing the righteous, one listing the wicked, and one listing those somewhere in between. Those in the first book are immediately inscribed for life; those in the second book for death; and those in the third book are given ten days to repent and perform enough good deeds to outweigh their bad deeds.

Rosh Hashanah is also known as the Day of the Sounding of the Shofar or the Feasts of Trumpets. God directed Moses in Numbers 10:1–10 to fashion two silver trumpets to be used to assemble the children of Israel, to announce the moving of the camps, to sound an alarm in battle, and to be used during the sacrificial offerings performed on festival days. Along with these two silver trumpets, a shofar (ram's horn) was blown on Rosh Hashanah. The shofar became the more prominent instrument on this day.

There is no reason given in Scripture for blowing the trumpets, other than as a "memorial" or reminder (Lev. 23:24). But a reminder to whom? Israel blew the two silver trumpets in battle and on festival days to "be remembered before the LORD [their] God" (Num. 10:9-10). Most likely that was also why they were blown on Rosh Hashanah—so that God would remember His covenant relationship with Israel and the promises He had made to them.

Jewish tradition, however, views blowing the shofar as more of a reminder to Israel than to God. On Rosh Hashanah the shofar reminds the Jewish people of two things.

First, it reminds them to offer their lives to God. The account of the offering of Isaac plays a major role on Rosh Hashanah and is highly regarded. Not only is it believed that the offering of Isaac occurred on Rosh Hashanah, but Isaac's willingness to be bound and put to death is seen as the greatest example for Jewish martyrdom—their readiness to be sacrificed for their beliefs. Also, when Israel remembers the offering of Isaac on Rosh

Hashanah, as well as the merits of all of the patriarchs (Abraham, Isaac, and Jacob), God grants them mercy on this day of judgment. It is said that when He hears the sound of the shofar, God is moved to leave His seat of judgment and go to His seat of mercy and forgiveness. As expressed in one of the prayers on Rosh Hashanah, "Do Thou heed from heaven's heights the Shofar-blast, and leave Thy throne of stern justice for Thy seat of mercy. Remember Isaac who was bound on the altar, and for his sake, grant his offspring mercy."[1]

Second, it reminds them to have faith in the future coming of the Messiah and the regathering of Israel back to their homeland (Isa. 27:13). As the high holiday prayer book states, "Our God and God of our fathers, sound the great Shofar for our freedom, set up the banner to gather our exiles, assemble our scattered ones from among the nations, and gather our dispersed from the uttermost parts of the earth."[2]

All of these reminders for God and Israel show why Rosh Hashanah is also known as the Day of Remembrance.

Observance of Rosh Hashanah

Rosh Hashanah is the only Jewish holiday celebrated on a new moon (the first of the month), in the month Tishri (September-October). Like other major Jewish festivals (except Yom Kippur), Rosh Hashanah is observed for an extra day, from Tishri 1 through Tishri 2. Even so, in Jewish teaching both days of Rosh Hashanah are regarded as one long day rather than two separate days.

The biblical directives for observing this holiday include a set of special offerings, in addition to the regular daily sacrifices and the sacrifices offered on the first of each month. Without a Temple, these sacrifices are no longer performed in Israel. Rosh Hashanah was also marked by the blowing of the trumpets, but this was not unusual, for on the first of every month throughout the year trumpets were blown over the monthly sacrifices as a memorial before God.

Rosh Hashanah was not unique from the first days of the other months because of the sacrifices or blowing the trumpets. Rather, it was the fact that it was a Sabbath day on which no work was permitted—a day of rest. Today, the work prohibition is still followed for both days.

In earlier times, the leaders of the Jewish communities fasted on the eve of Rosh Hashanah believing that their act would pardon one-third of Israel's sins. Between Rosh Hashanah and Yom Kippur other selected people also fasted, thus earning the pardon of one-third more of Israel's sins. Finally, on the Day of Atonement everyone fasted, wiping out the remaining third of Israel's sins.

Today fasting is not common on Rosh Hashanah. Instead, hearty meals are eaten, with an emphasis on sweet foods, symbolizing the hope for a sweet new year. On the first night of the holiday, a piece of hallah (festival bread) is dipped in honey and eaten. This is followed by the dipping of a slice of apple. A blessing is pronounced, along with a prayer, "May it be Your will to renew in our behalf a good and sweet year."[3] After the evening service on the first day of Rosh Hashanah, the worshipers greet each other with, "May you be inscribed and sealed immediately for a good life." Another commonly expressed variation of this greeting is, "May God inscribe you and your loved ones for a healthy and happy New Year!" This greeting is not expressed again during the two days of Rosh Hashanah. To do so would imply that the person being greeted has not already merited the inscription.

The highlight of the holiday is the blowing of the shofar. A shofar can be made from the horn of any animal except a cow, because of its association with the golden calf of Exodus 32. In

Temple days the shofar was made from the horn of a wild goat. It was straight, and its mouthpiece was overlaid with gold. The shofar was blown in Israel on occasions other than Rosh Hashanah. It was especially used during times of public distress. Blowing the shofar was looked upon as an act of crying out to God in time of great need. Today shofars come in various shapes and sizes.

The procedure for blowing the shofar is the same for both days of Rosh Hashanah. Before it is sounded, Psalm 47 is recited seven times. During the course of the festival, the horn must be blown a minimum of nine blasts, three sets each of a sustained blast, a quavering blast, and another sustained blast. In biblical times the sound of the shofar blowing in the Temple Court could be heard all the way to Jericho.

On the first day of Rosh Hashanah, following the afternoon service, Orthodox congregants go to the nearest body of water (an ocean, river, stream, or even a well) and empty their pockets into the water. Some people throw in bread crumbs or stones. This practice is based on Micah 7:18–19 and is said to symbolize the intent of the worshipers' hearts to cast away their sin and "achieve total purification from its effect."[4] This ritual is known as *Tashlich* (lit., *You shall cast*). It is a ritual of somewhat recent origin, not having been observed before the 13th century. In the 14th century, Jewish people were falsely accused of poisoning the wells of Europe through the ceremony of Tashlich, and they were subsequently blamed for causing the Black Death (bubonic plague).

Other common modern practices during the two days of Rosh Hashanah include sending New Year's greeting cards, wearing the festival garment known as the *kittel*, and, on the second day, adding a new fruit at meal time or wearing a new garment.

Prophecy and Rosh Hashanah

On Wednesday, June 7, 1967, at the height of the Six-Day War, Israeli forces pushed into Jerusalem and recaptured the Temple Mount. After two thousand years, the Jewish people's holiest place was once again in their possession. At the Western Wall, the last vestige of the walls that once surrounded the ancient Temple, hardened soldiers wept openly in joy. Others gently embraced the rough stones that towered above them. The Chief Army Chaplain, Rabbi Schlomo Goren, then performed a very significant act: He sounded the shofar.

People familiar with the prophetic designs of the Feast of Rosh Hashanah immediately recognized the intent of Rabbi Goren. By blowing the shofar, he symbolically announced to the world Israel's return to the home of their forefathers. This is the prophetic message of Rosh Hashanah—the future return, restoration, or regathering of the people of Israel back to the land God has given to them.

In the Book of Deuteronomy Moses delivered his final charge to the people of Israel. They were told that if they disobeyed God's commands, the result would be global dispersion. A survey of Israel's history shows that God has been true to His Word. The nation did rebel against God and therefore suffered the terrible consequence of dispersion. As a result of the scattering in A.D. 70 by the Roman army, followed by another dispersion in A.D. 135, Jewish people were scattered to the four corners of the earth. Today Jewish people can be found in almost every country of the world.

In spite of their displacement from the land of promise, God has given the people of Israel His pledge that one day He will bring them back home.

And it shall come to pass, when all these things are come upon thee, the blessing and the curse, which I have set before thee, and thou shalt call them to mind among all the nations, to which the LORD thy God hath driven thee, And shalt return unto the LORD thy God, and shalt obey his voice according to all that I command thee this day, thou and thy children, with all thine heart, and with all thy soul, That then the LORD thy God will turn thy captivity, and have compassion upon thee, and will return and gather thee from all the nations where the LORD thy God hath scattered thee. If any of thine be driven out unto the outmost parts of heaven, from there will the LORD thy God gather thee, and from there will he fetch thee. And the LORD thy God will bring thee into the land which thy fathers possessed, and thou shalt possess it; and he will do thee good, and multiply thee above thy fathers. And the LORD thy God will circumcise thine heart, and the heart of thy seed, to love the LORD thy God with all thine heart, and with all thy soul, that thou mayest live (Dt. 30:1–6).

There are three main elements in this passage: Israel's repentance, Israel's regathering, and Israel's revival. These three components are also reiterated in numerous other prophetic texts. The order of end-time events in relationship to the nation of Israel can therefore be outlined as follows:

1. A partial return to the land in unbelief (see chapter on Yom ha-Atzma'ut).

2. Israel's repentance brought about by the Tribulation period and the revelation of Jesus Christ (Dt. 4:30; Zech. 12:10).

3. The Second Coming of Jesus Christ (Zech. 14:3–4).

4. The supernatural regathering of Israel, accompanied by the sound of the shofar (Mt. 24:31).

5. The judgment of Israel to purge out those who still refuse to believe in Jesus Christ (Ezek. 20:33–38).

6. The return of Israel to the land of promise (Ezek. 36:24; also foreshadowed by the Feast of Rosh Hashanah).

7. The cleansing of Israel and the gift of a new heart and a new spirit to all Jewish people (see chapter on Yom Kippur).

8. Israel will receive and enjoy the Kingdom blessings (Ezek. 36:33–38; Dan. 9:24; see chapter on Sukkot).

As with some of the other festivals, there is no clear indication in Scripture that Rosh Hashanah will be celebrated during the millennial reign of the Messiah Jesus. Because blowing the trumpets was to serve as a memorial or reminder to God of His covenant promises to Israel, there would be no reason to continue that reminder once the covenant promises are fulfilled. But it is also possible that Rosh Hashanah could be one of the feasts listed in Ezekiel 45:17 that will be observed during the Millennium. If so, it would most likely be to memorialize God's faithfulness in keeping His covenant promises.

ENDNOTES

[1] Rabbi Morris Silverman, comp., *High Holiday Prayer Book* (Hartford, CT: Prayer Book Press, 1951), 140.

[2] Ibid., 134.

[3] Eliyahu Kitov, *The Book of Our Heritage*, trans. Nathan Bulman, rev. ed., 3 vols. (Jerusalem: Feldheim Publishers, 1979), 1:28.

[4] *IBID.*, 56.

Prayer and fasting
during Yom Kippur

6

YOM KIPPUR:
THE DAY OF ATONEMENT

For the sin which we have committed before
Thee by unclean lips, and for the sin which we
have committed before Thee by impure speech;
for the sin which we have committed before
Thee by the evil inclination, and for the sin
which we have committed before Thee witting-
ly or unwittingly; for all these, O God of forgiveness, forgive us, pardon us, grant us atonement. In the book of life, blessing, peace and
good sustenance, may we be remembered and
inscribed before thee.[1]

These are but a few of the words recited by penitent wor-
shipers on the most important day of the Jewish calendar.
Sometimes called "The Great Day" or, even more reverentially,
"The Day," it is the solemn occasion on which a Jewish person's
fate is determined for the coming year. It is Yom Kippur—the
Day of Atonement.

Origin and Description of Yom Kippur

The Day of Atonement is a holy day established by God for the people of Israel (Lev. 16). Biblically, Yom Kippur was to provide an atonement (lit., *a covering*) for sin, for the holy of holies in the Tabernacle, for the Tabernacle itself, for the altar of incense in the holy place, for the priests (including the high priest), and for the sins committed in ignorance by the people of Israel. Yom Kippur was divinely ordained "because of the uncleanness of the children of Israel, and because of their transgressions in all their sins" (Lev. 16:16). An everlasting statute, it was the once-a-year, awe-inspiring zero hour for an impure nation, a nation that was required to stand clean before its holy God.

The most consequential facet attributed to the Day of Atonement in rabbinical teaching, however, is that it is the day on which God's judgment of an individual is sealed. Ten days before, on Rosh Hashanah (the civil New Year), it is believed that God decides whether or not a person's name is inscribed in the Book of Life. From Rosh Hashanah through Yom Kippur inclusively, the Ten Days of Penitence, a person is admonished to sincerely repent. On Rosh Hashanah the greeting is, "May you be inscribed [in the Book of Life]," while on Yom Kippur the greeting is "May you be sealed [in the Book of Life]."

Observance of Yom Kippur

God instructed the children of Israel to observe the Day of Atonement on the tenth day of the seventh month. Today it is observed on the tenth day of the first month, Tishri (September-October). There is no discrepancy, however, because Tishri is the seventh month of the Jewish religious calendar; it is also the first month of the Jewish civil calendar. Unlike the other major Jewish festivals, Yom Kippur is observed for only one day, both inside and outside of Israel. Rabbinical authorities believed fasting for two days would be too great a physical hardship to impose, and they thus restricted the observance to one day.

The mood of Yom Kippur has changed over the years. Although solemn in modern practice, the day originally was characterized by joyful celebration. First, there was joy over the forgiveness of sins. Second, there was joy, at least among the eligible bachelors, over an interesting custom. On Yom Kippur all the Jewish maidens dressed in white garments and went to the vineyards, where they danced together. The young, single men looked on and chose the maidens they liked for future betrothals. Finally, Yom Kippur was a day of joy because every fifty years Israel celebrated the year of jubilee, during which all Jewish slaves were set free and the land itself enjoyed rest from cultivation. The blowing of the trumpet on the tenth day of the seventh month—Yom Kippur—proclaimed the year of jubilee (Lev. 25:8–12).

Along with performing various required sacrifices and offerings, all labor was forbidden on this day. God promised to destroy those who disobeyed this command. This warning was taken so seriously that, according to rabbinical law, if a person is injured by a falling building on Yom Kippur, the rescuers must be sure that the victim is still alive before he or she is removed. If the person is dead, the body is left until after Yom Kippur, so that the prohibition against work is not broken.

Another primary obligation of the people of Israel on Yom Kippur was to "afflict" their souls (Lev. 16:29). Mentioned six times in Scripture, this divine decree literally means that the people were to *humble* themselves. The idea is for people to put themselves in proper perspective, recognize their absolute spiritual bankruptcy, and acknowledge their total dependence on Almighty God. Thus, the Jewish people were expected to approach Yom Kippur, the day on which their sins were covered for another year by the awesome and exalted God of the universe, with humility of mind and soul. The children of Israel understood this command to afflict their souls in terms of abstinence, particularly abstinence from food. Thus, by the Second Temple days, fasting on Yom Kippur had become a common practice as the primary means of afflicting the soul, a custom that continues to this day and is fulfilled by a full 24 hours of fasting.

In preparation for the solemnity of Yom Kippur, weddings are not performed during the Ten Days of Penitence. Restitution between wronged individuals is advocated. Gifts are bestowed on the poor. When the day arrives, it is ushered in with the lighting of the customary holiday candles in the home. In some homes, additional candles are also lit in honor and memory of deceased relatives. It is a belief of some Jewish teachings that if people pray and give to charity on the Day of Atonement, along with lighting memorial candles, deceased parents will merit atonement, and their souls will ascend to a higher level in paradise.

Most of the activity on Yom Kippur occurs in the synagogue. In Orthodox congregations, the worshipers often wear white clothing. The men in particular wear a white garment called a kittel, the same garment worn on Passover. Also, unlike any other evening service, Jewish male worshipers don prayer shawls, or *tallitot* (plural of *tallit*).

Before sunset, the Yom Kippur opening synagogue service is introduced by singing the beloved *Kol Nidrei* (*All Vows*) prayer. Accompanied by a lovely melody, the lyrics declare null and void any personal vows people may rashly make between themselves and God during the course of the coming year (some say for the past year). A very old prayer dating back to the eighth century, the Kol Nidrei is chanted three times throughout the services on Yom Kippur.

The confession of sins is another significant and often-repeated segment of the Yom Kippur synagogue ritual. Ten times on Yom

Kippur worshipers rehearse a long list of sins recorded in the holiday prayer book, called the *Machzor*. The Machzor names specific sins and asks for forgiveness from them all.

> For the sin which we have committed before
> Thee by denying and lying, and for the sin
> which we have committed before Thee by
> bribery; for the sin which we have committed
> before Thee by scoffing, and for the sin which
> we have committed before Thee by slander; For
> the sin which we have committed before Thee
> in commerce, and for the sin which we have
> committed before Thee in eating and drinking;
> For the sin which we have committed before
> Thee by demanding usurious interest, and for
> the sin which we have committed before Thee
> by stretching forth the neck in pride; For the sin
> which we have committed before Thee by idle
> gossip, and for the sin which we have commit-
> ted before Thee with wanton looks; For the sin
> which we have committed before Thee with
> haughty eyes, and for the sin which we have
> committed before Thee by effrontery; *For all
> these, O God of forgiveness, forgive us, pardon
> us, grant us atonement.*[2]

As the worshipers repeat the string of iniquities outlined in their
prayer books, they beat their breasts with their hands, as if to say to
their hearts, "Your counsel and ruminations caused me to sin."[3]

Another central part of the liturgy on Yom Kippur is the
Avodah, which, along with various prayers and poems, recounts
the multifaceted duties of the high priest on the Day of
Atonement.   These duties, as outlined in Leviticus 16 and
expanded on in the Mishnah, comprise the bulk of the activities
on Yom Kippur in biblical times. They also serve as additional

brush strokes in the messianic portrait God painted through Israel and its festivals. An examination of the high priestly duties shows how atonement was procured under the law of Moses.

Preparation for the Atoning Work

Seven days before Yom Kippur, the high priest was taken aside and drilled on his assignments for that all-important day. As the evening of the tenth of Tishri approached, with its accompanying fast, the elders of the Sanhedrin started to deprive the high priest of food. The fast was started early because food induces sleep, and they wanted the high priest to stay awake all that night. The elders of the Sanhedrin then transferred the responsibility of watching the high priest that night to the elders of the priesthood. To insure that the high priest did not sleep, the other priests read to him from Scripture, snapped their fingers, or walked him on cold pavement.

By dawn, the Temple Court was filled to capacity with Jewish worshipers. As on all of the festivals, Roman soldiers were stationed around the Temple area, ready for action in the event of rioting by the multitude of worshipers. A linen sheet was hung on the roof of a chamber on the north side of the Temple Court, behind which the high priest changed his clothes and immersed himself in water five times. The high priest was keenly aware that, according to Jewish law, if he performed any of the Yom Kippur procedures out of the prescribed order, he would have to begin again from the point at which he erred.

Before the Day of Atonement sacrifices commenced, the high priest was required to fulfill the daily Temple obligations. In doing this, he removed his own personal clothing, immersed himself, and put on the gold garments made especially for his office. He then washed his hands and feet with water from a golden jug, sanctifying these extremities for service (an act he performed a total of ten times on that day). Next he sacrificed and offered the daily whole offering (Num. 28:1–8). He then burned the morning incense and trimmed the Temple lamps (Ex. 30:7), after which he again washed his hands and feet. Finally, he removed the gold garments, immersed himself, dressed in the required white linen garments for that day, and washed his hands and feet once more.

Atoning for the Priesthood

Now the high priest was ready to begin the special duties assigned for Yom Kippur. He placed his hands on the head of a bull that had been set aside as a sin offering for himself and his family, identifying the animal with his sins. He then recited this confession:

O God, I have committed iniquity, transgressed, and sinned before You, I and my house. O God, forgive the iniquities and transgressions and sins which I have committed and transgressed and sinned before You, I and my house, as it is written in the Law of Your servant Moses, "For on this day shall atonement be made for you to cleanse you: from all your sins shall you be clean before the Lord."

As the high priest ended the confession with the phrase "before the Lord," he spoke aloud the sacred name of God, the name Jehovah. Upon hearing the ineffable name of *Jehovah*, the mass of people responded by falling down on their faces in worship, proclaiming, "Blessed be the name of the glory of His kingdom for ever and ever!"

The high priest then approached two male goats that had been taken from the people, both of which were to be used as sin offerings. Their fates, however, were to be entirely different. Near the two goats, the high priest shook a small box containing two lots. On one lot were written the words, "For the Lord," and on the other lot, "For *Azazel*" (scapegoat). He put both hands in the box and took a lot in each hand. The hand with the lot "For the Lord" signified which goat would be sacrificed. The other lot signified which goat would be the scapegoat. The high priest then pronounced, "A sin offering to the Lord" (Jehovah), after which the people responded in worship as before. To distinguish between the two goats, the high priest tied a red wool thread or rope to the head of the scapegoat and a second rope to the neck of the sacrificial goat.

Returning to the bull set aside for a sin offering, the high priest again placed his hands on the animal and made the same confession over it as he had done previously, uttering for the third time the holy name of Jehovah. Again the people responded in worship, "Blessed be the name of the glory of His kingdom for ever and ever!" The high priest then slaughtered the bull and caught its blood in a bowl, which he gave to a nearby priest who stirred the blood to keep it from coagulating. Next the high priest scooped out coals from the bronze altar.[4] With a ladle containing two handfuls of incense in his left hand and a fire pan of coals in his right hand, he entered the sanctuary or holy place of the Temple.

Passing the table of showbread on his right and the golden seven-branched candlestick on his left, the high priest went behind the veil into the holy of holies. Putting the fire pan down between the two poles of the ark of the covenant, he powdered the coals with the incense. The resulting smoke filled the room. After burning the incense, he exited the holy of holies, said a short prayer in the holy place, and went to retrieve the blood of the bull. He did not dawdle in the holy place, lest the congregation be frightened and think he had been struck down by God.

With the bull's blood in hand, the high priest entered the holy of holies again and, with his finger, sprinkled the mercy seat with the blood. He counted as he flung the blood once upward and seven times downward. This act completed, the high priest left the holy of holies and deposited the basin of blood in the holy place.

Atoning for the Holy of Holies, the Tabernacle, and the Altar

The high priest then sacrificed the male goat chosen by lot and designated "For the Lord." Unlike the bull, he did not pronounce a priestly confession of the goat. Once the animal was slain, its blood was carried into the holy of holies by the high priest, and the same sprinkling procedure as with the bull's blood was performed. Following that, the basin was brought into the holy place.

Picking up the basin of bull's blood, the high priest again sprinkled the blood as he had done in the holy of holies, this time sprinkling it on the veil separating the two compartments. He did the same with the blood of the goat. Then he mixed the remaining blood of the bull with that of the goat. Going to the altar of incense (Ex. 30:10), he sprinkled some of the mixed blood on the four horns of the altar, beginning with the northeast horn and working counterclockwise to the southeast horn. Finally he sprinkled the top of the altar seven times, exited, and poured what was left of the blood at the base of the bronze altar.

Atoning for All of the People of Israel

Now it was time for one of the most unusual yet fascinating rituals performed on the Day of Atonement—the scapegoat. Approaching the male goat with the red wool thread tied to its head, the high priest laid his hands on it and recited the same confession of sins as he pronounced over the bull, the only exception being the substitution of the House of Israel for himself and his own house. Within the confession, the holy name of God—Jehovah—was spoken for the fourth time that day, and the people reacted as before, falling down and blessing God.

The goat was then led away and drawn across a special causeway by a priest chosen for the task. The priest took the goat a distance of approximately 12 miles into the wilderness, stopping at ten booths or stations along the way for food and drink. After the last station, the priest brought the scapegoat to a ravine where he tied one end of the red wool thread or rope to a rock and the other end to the goat's horns. The priest then pushed the goat over the edge and into the ravine, killing it. The priest, who was then unclean by reason of his duty with the scapegoat, remained at the last station until nightfall, at which time he could return.

When the scapegoat had been destroyed, the news was relayed back to the Temple by a series of sentinels waving flags. Meanwhile, the high priest burned the sacrificial parts of the sin offering of the bull and goat on the bronze altar. Unlike most sin offerings, these were not eaten by the priests (Lev. 6:24–30). Instead, the remains of the carcasses were taken outside of the city of Jerusalem and burned by designated people (who became temporarily unclean).

Sequel to the Atoning Work

As the animal remains were being burnt, the high priest stood and read portions of Scripture to the people. Following the reading, he pronounced eight benedictions, after which he washed his hands and feet again, removed his linen clothing, and immersed himself. Then he redressed in the gold high priestly garments, washed his hands and feet, and sacrificed the two rams designated for a burnt offering[5], along with some of the extra offerings prescribed for that day.

Following this ritual, he again washed his hands and feet, removed the gold vestments, immersed again, put on the linen garments once more, and again washed his hands and feet. The high priest then returned to the holy of holies and retrieved the ladle and fire pan he had left there earlier in the day. Following that, he again went through the ritual of washing his hands and feet, stripping off the linen clothes, bathing, putting on the gold garments, and washing his hands and feet.

Returning to the holy place, the high priest burned the afternoon incense and trimmed the Temple lamps. Then, for the last time, he washed his hands and feet, removed the gold garments, and put on his own personal clothes, bringing to a conclusion his exhaustive duties for Yom Kippur. To celebrate the fact that he had not been struck down by the Lord, the high priest ended the day quietly at home, enjoying a splendid feast with his family and friends.

Thus, the Yom Kippur observance in biblical days centered primarily around the high priest and the services he performed in the Temple. The responsibilities of the children of Israel on this day were few because they were to abstain from work and were to humble their souls (misguidedly relegated to simple fasting).

Today much has changed. Atonement on Yom Kippur is no longer viewed in terms of national cleansing, as spelled out in Scripture. Rather, Yom Kippur now focuses more on individual, personal atonement. The shift in perspective came with the destruction of Jerusalem by the Romans in A.D. 70. With no Temple, no priesthood, no sacrifices, and the worldwide dispersion of the Jews, finding a way to be cleansed from sins became a problem.

Some Orthodox groups employ a ninth-century ritual called *Kapparot* (*Expiations*). On the day preceding Yom Kippur, a chicken is swung three times over the head of a penitent sinner as a prayer is recited: "This is my substitute, my vicarious offering, my atonement; this cock [for males, a hen for females] shall meet death, but I shall find a long and pleasant life of peace."[6]

The predominant view in modern rabbinical Judaism is that sin is now atoned for by means of prayer, repentance, and good deeds. There is no need for a vicarious, substitutionary atonement because people are not viewed as suffering from original sin. Rather, people start life with a pure soul (as stated each day in the morning prayer: "O my God, the soul which Thou gavest me is pure"[7]), and they must struggle all their lives to keep it pure. Therefore, as one Jewish leader declared, "Judaism does not throw the burden of its sins on other shoulders, and it does not let the innocent expiate the actions of the guilty. In Judaism, there is no vicarious atonement. One's own guilt—one's own punishment; no pardon without true repentance."[8] Apart from prayer, repentance, and good deeds, modern Judaism also teaches that personal suffering may pay for sin. Even death is sufficient suffering to obtain atonement. The dying person is encouraged to proclaim, "May my death be an atonement for all my sins."[9]

Without the Temple, priesthood, or sacrifices, punishment for sin can be avoided and atonement procured within modern Judaism in the following manner:

1. Repentance atones.
2. If there is a more serious sin, repentance postpones the punishment and the Day of Atonement atones.
3. If there is an even more serious sin, repentance and the Day of Atonement postpone, and suffering atones.
4. If there is a grave sin, such as profaning God's name, repentance, the Day of Atonement, and suffering all postpone the punishment, while death provides the atonement.

Prophecy and Yom Kippur

A prophetic examination of the Day of Atonement is the key to understanding how God has provided final atonement, not only for the sins of Israel but for those of the world. Modern Judaism would agree with the Christian teaching that, according to Leviticus 16, it was God who provided atonement for Israel. A parting of the ways occurs, however, over whether God used the medium of the high priest to accomplish that atonement. Judaism teaches that other religions, such as Christianity, need a mediator, while Judaism does not.

This view is contrary to the evidence in the Scriptures. Biblical Judaism has always known intermediaries—those who went to God on Israel's behalf. Moses interceded for Israel on numerous occasions (Ex. 32:30–32). The Levites were chosen specifically to be the instruments through which God would make atonement for Israel (Num. 8:19). The office of high priest was ordained with the same purpose in mind (Lev. 9:7). Leviticus 16:32–33 makes it clear that on the Day of Atonement, the high priest was responsible for making atonement for the nation of Israel. Of course, only God can forgive sin, but He chose to use the high priesthood as the agency through which forgiveness was supplied. With this truth in mind, we see why God eventually provided the supreme liaison between Himself and mankind: "For there is one God, and one mediator between God and men, the man, Christ Jesus" (1 Tim. 2:5).

The Book of Hebrews explains in detail how Jesus the Messiah is *better* or *greater* in His priesthood and sacrifice than the Old Testament Levitical priesthood and sacrifice. The following charts illustrate this.

Levitical Priesthood	Scripture Reference	Messiah's Priesthood
Levi gave tithes to Melchizedek, thus demonstrating the superiority of Melchizedek's priesthood.	Hebrews 5:6; 7:4–10	Jesus was a priest according to the order of Melchizedek.
Levitical priests became priests on the basis of a physical birthright.	Hebrews 7:16	Jesus became a priest on the merits of an endless life.

Levitical Priesthood	Scripture Reference	Messiah's Priesthood
Levitical priests became priests only by the law of Moses.	Hebrews 7:21, 28	Jesus became a priest with an oath from God.
The Levitical priesthood required large numbers.	Hebrews 7:23–24	The Messiah's priesthood needed only one priest.
Levitical priests died.	Hebrews 7:23–24	Jesus lives forever.
Levitical priests were prevented from continuing their ministry.	Hebrews 7:23–24	Jesus holds His priesthood permanently.
A Levitical priest's atoning intermediacy was temporary, ending at his death.	Hebrews 7:23, 25	Jesus is able to save forever, since He always lives to intercede.
The high priest exchanged only his clothes to provide atonement.	Leviticus 16:4; Hebrews 2:9, 14, 17; Philippians 2:5–7	Jesus exchanged His glory to provide atonement.
Levitical priests had to offer sacrifices for themselves.	Hebrews 7:26–27	Jesus was sinless and needed no sacrifice for Himself.
Levitical priests had to offer sacrifices repeatedly.	Hebrews 7:27	Jesus offered a once-for-all sacrifice.
Levitical priests were mere men.	Hebrews 7:28	Jesus is the Son of God, made perfect for evermore.
Levitical priests had to stand while ministering because their work was never finished.	Hebrews 10:11–12; 1:3; 8:1	Jesus sat down at the right hand of God because His atoning work was completed.

The writer of Hebrews confronts his readers with this probing question. "If, therefore, perfection were by the Levitical priesthood…what further need was there that another priest should rise after the order of Melchizedek, and not be called after the order of Aaron?" (Heb. 7:11; cp. Ps. 110:4). The answer is self-evident: Because the Levitical priesthood was deficient in that it could never provide lasting atonement from sin, a superior priesthood was needed—one allocated to the Messiah and fulfilled in the person of Jesus Christ.

Old Testament Sacrifice	Scripture Reference	Messiah's Sacrifice
The Old Testament place of atonement was an earthly Tabernacle.	Hebrews 9:1–7, 11, 24	The Messiah's place of atonement is a heavenly Tabernacle.
The Old Testament place of atonement was a Tabernacle pitched by man.	Hebrews 8:2	The Messiah's place of atonement is a Tabernacle pitched by God.
The Old Testament place of atonement was a mere copy.	Hebrews 8:5; 9:24	The Messiah's place of atonement is the original —heaven itself.
The Old Testament sacrifices cleansed the Tabernacle on earth.	Hebrews 9:23	The Messiah's sacrifice cleansed the Tabernacle in heaven.[10]
The Old Testament sacrifices used the blood of animals.	Hebrews 9:13–14	The Messiah's sacrifice was His own blood.
The Old Testament sacrifices could only cover (atone) sins.	Hebrews 9:9, 26; 10:1–4, 11, 14	As illustrated by the scapegoat, the Messiah's sacrifice took away sins completely.
The remains of the Old Testament Yom Kippur sin offerings were always burnt outside the camp, showing a separation from and a rejection by the community of Israel; the Yom Kippur offerings were mere animals.	Leviticus 16:27; Hebrews 13:11–12; John 1:11	Jesus also suffered outside the gate, showing a separation from and a rejection by the people of Israel, although He was the Messiah.

Old Testament Sacrifice	Scripture Reference	Messiah's Sacrifice
The Old Testament sacrifices had to be repeated every year.	Hebrews 9:25–26, 28; 10:1, 10, 12	The Messiah's one sacrifice was for all time.

Using Yom Kippur as a type, God presented a picture of His Son—the ultimate atonement, accomplished through the ultimate high priest, at a price of ultimate sacrifice.

Yom Kippur bears significance to the Messiah's first coming as well as to His Second Coming. For the nation of Israel, the final atonement has been accomplished, but its efficacy has not yet been applied. Israel's high priest, the Messiah Jesus, is prophetically still within the holy of holies, His own blood being presented before God as the propitiation for the sins of the whole world (1 Jn. 2:2).

When Jesus returns, however, it will not be to procure atonement for sins. Rather, it will be to provide salvation for Israel and for all those who eagerly await Him (Heb. 9:28). Just as the people of Israel anxiously awaited the reappearance of the high priest from the holy of holies on the Day of Atonement, signifying that God was satisfied with the atoning sacrifice, so too will Jesus reappear in the heavens, having satisfied God's righteous demands for a perfect, once-for-all cleansing from sin. Israel will be washed clean, given a new heart, and will receive God's indwelling Spirit (Ezek. 36:25–27). "In that day there shall be a fountain opened to the house of David and to the inhabitants of Jerusalem for sin and for uncleanness" (Zech. 13:1). "And so [or, in this manner] all Israel shall be saved; as it is written, There shall come out of Zion the Deliverer, and shall turn away ungodliness from Jacob; For this is my covenant unto them, when I shall take away their sins" (Rom. 11:26–27).

The Bible does not mention the observance of Yom Kippur during the reign of the Messiah on earth because there will no longer be a need to keep the Day of Atonement. The final sacrifice will have already been paid. As the Scriptures teach, "Now where remission of these is, there is no more offering for sin" (Heb. 10:18). If, however, Yom Kippur is part of the millennial holy days (Ezek. 45:17), it will most likely serve as an object lesson of what Jesus Christ has already accomplished.

ENDNOTES

[1] Rabbi Morris Silverman, comp., *High Holiday Prayer Book* (Hartford, CT: Prayer Book Press, 1951), 271, 269.

[2] Ibid., 222–223.

[3] Eliyahu Kitov, *The Book of Our Heritage*, trans. Nathan Bulman, rev. ed., 3 vols. (Jerusalem: Feldheim Publishers, 1978), 1:104.

[4] The Mishnah's account of scooping the coals from the bronze altar seems to differ from that of the biblical directive in Leviticus 16:12. The biblical text states that the coals were to be taken from the "altar before the LORD," which most probably refers to the altar of incense (cp. Ex. 30:10; Lev. 4:7, 18).

[5] The Mishnah reverses the biblical order. The Bible specifies sacrificing the burnt offerings before burning the sacrificial parts of the sin offerings (Lev. 16:24–25).

[6] *Encyclopaedia Judaica*, 16 vols. (Jerusalem: Keter Publishing House Ltd., 1971), 10:756–757.

[7] Joseph H. Hertz, *The Authorised Daily Prayer Book*, rev. ed. (New York: Bloch Publishing Co., 1948), 19.

[8] *Ibid.*, p. 906, quoting Nahida Remy.

[9] *The Mishnah*, trans. Herbert Danby (New York: Oxford University Press, 1933), Sanhedrin 6.2.

[10] People may wonder why heaven would need cleansing. Some have proposed that the cleansing is necessary due to Satan's rebellion there and that it is part of the reconciling of "all things," even the "things in heaven" (Col. 1:20).

A Sukkah is built in preparation for Sukkot, The Harvest Festival

7

SUKKOT:
THE FEAST OF TABERNACLES

He who dwelleth in the secret place of the Most High shall abide under the shadow of the Almighty. I will say of the LORD, He is my refuge and my fortress, my God; in him will I trust (Ps. 91:1–2).

The words of this beautiful psalm capture the essence of one of Israel's most beloved holidays. Considered the greatest of all the feasts, it is sometimes referred to simply as "The Holiday" or "The Feast." Filled with joyful memories of yesterday and hopeful dreams for tomorrow, this marvelous festival is known as Sukkot or the Feast of Tabernacles.

Origin and Description of Sukkot

The Feast of Tabernacles is the last in a series of God-ordained festivals given to Israel (Lev. 23:33–43). Sukkot was also the third and final occasion on which all Jewish adult males were required to make a pilgrimage to Jerusalem to appear before the Lord.

A joyful holiday filled with celebration, Sukkot also is known in Scripture as the Feast of Ingathering because it was held at the end of the harvest season, when God's bounty and provision were so clearly in view (Ex. 23:16). The Feast of Tabernacles had a commemorative purpose as well. It looked back to the time when the children of Israel dwelled in temporary shelters or booths as God led them through the wilderness and provided for their every need. The festival also has a prophetic aspect. One day, during the age of the Messiah, the glory of God representing the presence of God will again dwell with Israel as it once did in the wilderness.

Observance of Sukkot

Scripture mandated that the Feast of Tabernacles was to begin on the 15th day of the seventh month, Tishri (September-October), and last for seven days. The eighth day was a solemn assembly called *Shemini Atzeret*. No labor was permitted on the first or eighth days of the festival.

The Bible records that the Feast of Tabernacles was observed at the dedication of the Temple in the days of Solomon (1 Ki. 8:1–3, 65–66); at the time of Jeroboam, creator of a counterfeit Feast of Tabernacles (1 Ki. 12:32–33); during the first year of the returned exiles under Ezra (Ezra 3:4); during the governorship of Nehemiah, which was the first time since the days of Joshua that the people celebrated the feast by living in booths (Neh. 8:13–18); and during the ministry of Jesus (Jn. 7:10–11).

Numbers 29:12–39 outlines a certain number of animals to be offered as sacrifices during the seven days of Sukkot. Today, these animal sacrifices are no longer performed because there is no longer a Temple in Jerusalem. Apart from the work prohibition and the festival offerings, there were only three requirements prescribed for the holiday of Sukkot: the building of a temporary shelter or booth; the taking of four species of foliage; and rejoicing during all seven days.

Later two man-made customs were added. The first, not observed today, was the rite of water libation. A key element in the ritual of Sukkot by the time of Jesus, this ceremony was believed to have been given to Moses at Mount Sinai as part of the Oral Law handed down from generation to generation. The other addition to Sukkot is the waving of willow branches on the seventh day of the festival, which is still performed today.

Of all the requirements surrounding Sukkot, the most conspicuous is building the temporary shelter or booth called a *sukkah*. Observant Jews who participate in this custom sometimes begin building their booths immediately after Yom Kippur, hoping to gain merit with God. Booths are built at homes and often at synagogues. In Israel, it is common to find booths located on rooftops, balconies, and in courtyards. According to rabbinical teaching, the booth must meet a certain "building code" to be acceptable. It must be at least four feet long, four feet wide, no more than 30 feet high, and have at least three sides. Its roof is often covered with enough leaves and straw to provide shade without blocking out the view of the stars at night. The booth is decorated as attractively as possible. To fulfill the scriptural requirement of *dwelling* in their booths, holiday observers must spend more time in their booths during the week of the feast than in their homes. They are encouraged to have all of their meals during the feast inside the booths. On the first night of the feast, eating in the booth is obligatory.

The other prominent custom of the Feast of Tabernacles is the four species of foliage, which include the *etrog* (citrus fruit), the myrtle branch, the willow branch, and the palm branch called the *lulav*. The term *lulav* is also applied collectively to all three leafy branches. The myrtle, willow, and palm branches are bound together and held in the right hand, while the etrog is held in the left hand to be waved at the appropriate time.

One of the more fascinating man-made customs that developed in the liturgy of the Feast of Tabernacles was the rite of the water libation. No longer practiced today, the water libation became one of the most popular aspects of the feast during the time of the Second Temple. Every day for seven days, a priest would walk up the ramp leading to the bronze altar located in the Temple Court and pour a jug full of water into a bowl that drained into the altar. The significant thing about this ceremony was the place from which the water was drawn and the spiritual meaning applied to the rite itself.

The water was taken from a spring just to the east of the city of Jerusalem called the Spring of Gihon. It was here that David's son, Solomon, was anointed king of Israel (1 Ki. 1:45). King Hezekiah later redirected the water of this spring into the city of Jerusalem through a long underground conduit called Hezekiah's Tunnel (2 Chr. 32:30). This tunnel can be seen in Jerusalem today. Within the walls of Jerusalem, the waters of Gihon ran into a pool called the Pool of Siloam. Water from the Pool of Siloam was used in the ordinance of the red heifer described in Numbers 19, where Moses was instructed to mix "running" (lit., living) water with the ashes of a red heifer. The water had to be fresh, able to give and sustain life, not stagnant. This mixture of water and ashes was sprinkled on those who had become unclean to purify them. The Pool of Siloam is also referred to in the New Testament. It was to the pool that the Lord Jesus sent a man, blind from birth, to wash off the clay that He had applied to the man's eyes. After washing in the pool, the man received his sight (Jn. 9:6–7).

The Pool of Siloam not only held historical significance, but in Jewish tradition it also had a prophetic connotation. First, the Scriptures speak of a time when, like water poured "upon him that is thirsty, and floods upon the dry ground," God will pour out His Spirit upon all flesh (Isa. 44:3). Because the waters of Siloam were used to anoint the kings of the house of David, and that anointing was symbolic of the Holy Spirit coming upon an individual (1 Sam. 16:13), the living waters of Siloam became associated with the outpouring of the Holy Spirit. Second, this out pouring is to take place during the days of the Messiah, the Anointed One, a descendant of King David, through whom salvation will come to Israel. Based on Isaiah 12:3, the Pool of Siloam became known as the "well of salvation" and was associated with the messianic age. Thus, to the Jewish people of the Second Temple days, pouring water on the altar at the Feast of Tabernacles was symbolic of the Holy Spirit poured out during the days of the Messiah.

One reason the water libation ritual was so popular in Second Temple days was the accompanying ceremony of the water drawing, which took place at night when water was drawn from Siloam for the next morning's water libation. The ceremony of the water drawing was a jubilant occasion. The Mishnah states, "He that never has seen the joy of the [ceremony of the water drawing] has never in his life seen joy" (Sukkah 5.1). As the ceremony took place, Levites played lyres, trumpets, harps, cymbals, and other instruments, while other Levites sang. In the Temple area, three golden candlesticks nearly 75 feet high were lit by young boys climbing tall ladders, and the light from these candlesticks could be seen throughout all Jerusalem. Respected men of faith danced and sang in front of these candlesticks while carrying burning torches. As the ceremony progressed through the night, the priests blew the shofar three times. In the manner of the text of Isaiah 12:3, "Therefore, with joy shall ye draw water out of the wells of salvation," the evening was characterized by exuberant joy. It was a wonderful occasion that no one wanted to miss.

There is another man-made custom associated with Sukkot and practiced during the time of the Second Temple. The Temple priests attached willow branches to the sides of the bronze altar, bending them over the top. They then marched around the altar once as the shofar was blown, all the while reciting, "Save now, I beseech thee, O LORD! O LORD, I beseech thee, send now prosperity!" (Ps. 118:25). The people shook the lulavs they held in their hands at the beginning and end of the recitation of Psalm 118 and also at the beginning of verse 25. This ritual was repeated for the first six days of the feast. On the seventh day the priests marched around the altar seven times.

This seventh day of the festival is known as *Hoshana Raba*, or the Great Hosanna, derived from the first Hebrew word of Psalm 118:25. Today on Hoshana Raba, as Psalm 118:25 is chanted, the worshipers carry willow branches seven times around the *bema* (the platform where the Torah scroll is read) and beat them on the ground five times.

The eighth day of Sukkot, Shemini Atzeret, is really a festival unto itself. On this day in Israel (the ninth day in the Diaspora), the festival of Simchat Torah is observed (see the chapter on *Simchat Torah* for a fuller discussion).

Also, during Temple days, at the beginning of every eighth year, in accordance with Deuteronomy 31:10–13, the king of Israel read aloud selected passages from the Book of Deuteronomy to all the people in the Temple Court. This was done to expose the people to the Word of God and remind them of their covenant relationship with Him.

Prophecy and Sukkot

There is no doubt that the festival of Sukkot has a prophetic theme. In both biblical and rabbinical teachings, the Feast of Tabernacles typifies the days of the Messiah. It speaks of the future raising up of "the tabernacle of David that is fallen" (Amos 9:11); that is, the reestablishment of the kingly line of David. At that time, the Messiah will sit on David's throne and rule the earth with a rod of iron, and Israel will dwell in safety.

There is yet another aspect of Sukkot's prophetic intent. In Jewish tradition it is held that the "booths" that God spoke of in Leviticus 23:43 were not just the temporary shelters in which Israel dwelt as they journeyed through the wilderness. God was also referring to the "clouds of glory," the "sukkah of God," that overshadowed Israel. Sometimes referred to as the "Shekinah," these "clouds of glory" speak of the pillar of cloud by day and the pillar of fire by night that rested over the Tabernacle in Numbers 9:15-23, the cloud that filled the Temple in 2 Chronicles 5:13-14, and the glory that gradually left the Temple Mount in Ezekiel's day, finally resting on the Mount of Olives (Ezek. 10-11). In the wilderness, the Shekinah was used both as a covering and as a light (Ps. 105:39). It was also looked upon as a place where God dwelled (2 Chr. 6:1). Through the Shekinah glory, God "tabernacled" among the children of Israel.

The prophetic message of the Feast of Tabernacles conveys that the messianic age will be a time when the Shekinah glory of God, representing the presence of God, will once again dwell with Israel.

It is also worth noting that the Feast of Tabernacles is referred to repeatedly in the New Testament as proof of the messianic credentials of Jesus of Nazareth. John 1:14 says, "And the Word [referring to Jesus Christ] was made flesh, and dwelt among us (and we beheld his glory, the glory as of the only begotten of the

Father), full of grace and truth." The Greek word for *dwelt* used here means to *dwell as in a tabernacle or tent, to abide in a temporary shelter.* The meaning of this word along with the reference to "the glory" and an understanding of the typology of the Feast of Tabernacles makes it clear that John had a messianic meaning in mind. As the Messiah, Jesus is "the brightness of his [God's] glory" (Heb. 1:3). In Him the presence of God literally "tabernacled" among us.

With the same intent, Luke recorded an account in his Gospel to show that Jesus is the Messiah. Jesus is the King, and accompanying the King are the characteristics of a kingdom, which are portrayed in the Feast of Tabernacles. The imagery of Sukkot is unfolded through the use of such words as "glory," "tabernacles," "cloud," and "overshadowed."

> *But I tell you of a truth, There are some standing here, who shall not taste of death, till they see the kingdom of God. And it came to pass, about eight days after these sayings, that he [Jesus] took Peter and John and James, and went up into a mountain to pray. And as he prayed, the appearance of his countenance was altered, and his raiment was white and glistening. And, behold, there talked with him two men, who were Moses and Elijah, Who appeared in glory, and spoke of his decease which he should accomplish at Jerusalem. But Peter, and they that were with him, were heavy with sleep; and when they were awake, they saw his glory, and the two men that stood with him. And it came to pass, as they departed from him, that Peter said unto Jesus, Master, it is good for us to be here; let us make three booths: one for thee, and one for Moses, and one for Elijah, not knowing what he*

*said. While he thus spoke, there came a cloud, and
overshadowed them; and they feared as they
entered into the cloud. And there came a voice out
of the cloud, saying, This is my beloved Son; hear
him. And when the voice was past, Jesus was
found alone. And they kept it close, and told no
man in those days any of those things which they
had seen* (Lk. 9:27–36).

John 7 is even more obvious in its messianic tenor. In this portion of Scripture, Jesus of Nazareth not only observed the holiday
of Sukkot, he also used the festival as an illustration for His messianic claims.

*Now the Jews' feast of tabernacles was at hand.
His brethren, therefore, said unto him, Depart
from here, and go into Judea, that thy disciples
also may see the works that thou doest. For there
is no man that doeth anything in secret, and he
himself seeketh to be known openly. If thou do
these things, show thyself to the world. For neither did his brethren believe in him* (Jn. 7:2–5).

Although uttered in unbelief, the challenge of Jesus' brothers
was, humanly speaking, the most logical thing to do. Hundreds
of thousands of Jewish pilgrims from all around the world would
be at the Feast of Tabernacles in Jerusalem. If Jesus was claim-
ing to be the Messiah, what better opportunity would there be to
present Himself as such than at the feast that had so many inher-
ent messianic implications?

*Then Jesus said unto them, My time is not yet
come; but your time is always ready. The world
cannot hate you; but me it hateth, because I testi-
fy of it, that its works are evil. Go ye up unto this*

*feast. I go not up yet unto this feast; for my time
is not yet fully come. When he had said these
words unto them, he abode still in Galilee. But
when his brethren were gone up, then went he also
up unto the feast, not openly, but as it were in
secret* (Jn. 7:6–10).

The Lord's response to His brothers was not a fabrication. He
had to go to the feast; otherwise, He would be disobeying
Scripture. But He was not going in the manner that they
desired—with pomp and ceremony, fulfilling their expectations
of a victorious Messiah. The time for that had not yet come.
Instead, He went to the feast quietly, not with great miracles,
wonders, or proofs. Jesus wanted people to receive Him as
Messiah not on mere outward manifestations but rather on His
Word. Those who did so would have true faith.

Once the festival commenced, the people began to look for
Jesus (Jn. 7:11–13). But it was not until the middle of the feast,
after the booths had been erected, the opening Sabbath had
passed, and the excitement of the first water-drawing ceremony
had waned, that Jesus went into the Temple and began to teach
those who would listen (v. 14). The authorities marveled at His
grasp of the Scriptures because He had no formal, ministerial
education (v. 15). Jesus used the occasion to declare that He was
sent from God; that by healing a man on the Sabbath He had actually fulfilled the law, not broken it; and that shortly He would be
leaving them to go back to His Father (vv. 16-24, 28–29, 33–36).
As a result of this discourse, many Jewish people believed that
Jesus was the Messiah (v. 31)—so many, in fact, that the Jewish
religious leaders felt it necessary to send a band of Temple officers to arrest Him (v. 32). Instead, the officers returned empty-
handed, amazed themselves at Christ's teaching (vv. 45–46).

Finally, on the last day of the feast, Hoshana Raba, the climax of the entire week, Jesus made His greatest proclamation. "In the last day, that great day of the feast, Jesus stood and cried out, saying, If any man thirst, let him come unto me, and drink. He that believeth on me, as the scripture hath said, out of his heart shall flow rivers of living water" (Jn. 7:37–38).

This was no statement secretly whispered in a dark corner. The text says that Jesus "stood" to make His announcement, and He "cried," meaning that He spoke with a loud voice. He wanted everyone to hear the good news. The stunned crowd did hear, and they knew what He meant. To the first century Jewish mind, pouring the water on the altar at the Feast of Tabernacles symbolized the pouring out of the Holy Spirit in the days of the Messiah. Jesus was therefore declaring that He was the Messiah, and everyone who would believe in Him would receive the gift of the Holy Spirit, the "living water," not measured in terms of a trickling spring, the Spring of Gihon, but a flowing river—even numerous rivers!

The multitude's understanding the Lord's pronouncement is confirmed in the next three verses of John's account. "(But this spoke he of the Spirit, whom they that believe on him should receive; for the Holy Spirit was not yet given, because Jesus was not yet glorified.) Many of the people, therefore, when they heard this saying, said, Of a truth this is the Prophet. Others said, This is the Christ" (Jn. 7:39–41a).[1]

One other incident, often referred to as Jesus' triumphal entry, highlights the messianic undertones of the Feast of Tabernacles. Recorded in all four Gospels, this was the day when, in fulfillment of prophecy (Zech. 9:9), Jesus rode into Jerusalem, mounted on a donkey, as the King of Israel. As Jesus approached Jerusalem, the crowd, although they had gathered for the upcoming Passover festival, responded to Jesus as if it were Sukkot because with the Messiah's arrival they anticipated the subsequent kingdom blessings—blessings symbolized in the holiday of Tabernacles.

John 12:13 records that the people "Took branches of palm trees, and went forth to meet him." Matthew and Mark state that these branches were strewn across Jesus' path as He rode toward the city (Mt. 21:8; Mk. 11:8). Mark's account of these branches is particularly interesting. The text says, "And many spread their garments in the way; and others cut down branches off the trees, and spread them in the way." In the original Greek, the text states that these branches had been cut off of trees from "the fields."

What is the importance of stating that the branches were from trees in the field? The answer is found in rabbinical law. There are specific requirements for acceptable lulavs used at Sukkot. The law states that if a particular branch is not found by a brook (as in Lev. 23:40), it is permissible to use it if it is found in an unirrigated, open field. Thus, the branches that the jubilant crowd waved and tossed were rabbinically acceptable to use at Sukkot as lulavs. So it was that with the intent of waving lulavs, the people of Israel cut down branches upon Jesus' triumphal entry, joyfully welcoming their messianic King.

Another indication that the multitude was thinking of Sukkot and the messianic age when they greeted Jesus was the cheer that rose from the crowds, "Hosanna to the Son of David!" (Mt. 21:9). "Blessed be the kingdom of our father, David, that cometh in the name of the Lord. Hosanna in the highest!" (Mk. 11:10). The word *Hosanna* is the first word of Psalm 118:25 and means, *Save now, I beseech Thee*. This phrase is repeated on the seventh and most important day of the Feasts of Tabernacles (Hoshana Raba), as the people wave their lulavs. It is with that perspective that the crowd took up the chant of "Hosanna." Calling Jesus the "Son of David" (a messianic title), they anticipated His bringing to Israel their ultimate salvation and resultant glorification.

Jesus would have done so had the Jewish religious leaders, representing the nation as a whole, received Him as the Messiah of Israel, which the people, and even the little children (Mt. 21:15), had christened Him to be. Sadly, the leaders did not listen to the people (Lk. 23:35). The New Testament makes it abundantly clear that Jesus not only celebrated the holiday of Sukkot, He was also its fulfillment.

The Bible gives some intriguing information about the Feast of Tabernacles in the future. The images surrounding Sukkot are used to describe a heavenly scene in Revelation 7.9-17. John saw "a great multitude" of Gentile martyrs who were slain during the time of judgment known as the Great Tribulation. In their hands they carried "palms" (v. 9). God, who "sitteth on the throne shall dwell among them" (v. 15, lit., "dwell above" or "over them" like a shelter or covering, as seen in v. 16). The Lamb, Jesus, shall also "lead them unto living fountains of waters" (v. 17).

Following the Great Tribulation, Jesus the Messiah will return to the earth. The Feast of Tabernacles will then take on more meaning to the nation of Israel than at any time in the history of the Jewish people, for the Lord will wash away "the filth of the daughters of Zion" and purge "the blood of Jerusalem" (Isa. 4:4). When the cleansing of Israel is completed,

> The LORD will create upon every dwelling place of Mount Zion, and upon her assemblies, a cloud and smoke by day, and the shining of a flaming fire by night; for upon all the glory shall be a defense [Heb., huppah or canopy]. And there shall be a tabernacle [Heb., sukkah] for a shadow in the daytime from the heat, and for a place of refuge, and for a covert from storm and from rain (Isa. 4:5–6).

That for which Israel has yearned and longed when celebrating the Feast of Tabernacles will one day be fulfilled. The Shekinah glory of God (the cloud and the fire) will serve as a tabernacle over the Temple Mount, providing protection from the heat and refuge from the storm. The Messiah Himself will offer the sacrifices commensurate to the holiday (Ezek. 45:25). Most importantly, God's presence will return to Mount Zion. He will once again dwell among His people, never again to depart (cp. Ezek. 43:2–7).

The whole world will celebrate and observe the Feast of Tabernacles during the earthly reign of the Messiah:

> *And it shall come to pass that every one that is left of all the nations which came against Jerusalem shall even go up from year to year to worship the King, the LORD of hosts, and to keep the feast of tabernacles. And it shall be that whoever will not come up of all the families of the earth unto Jerusalem to worship the King, the LORD of hosts, even upon them shall be no rain. And if the family of Egypt go not up, and come not, that have no rain, there shall be the plague, with which the LORD will smite the nations that come not up to keep the feast of tabernacles. This shall be the punishment of Egypt, and the punishment of all nations that come not up to keep the feast of tabernacles* (Zech. 14:16–19).

Although nations will apparently have the option of whether or not to keep the holiday of Sukkot, to make the pilgrimage to Jerusalem, and to worship the King, there will be a negative consequence for making the wrong choice. That consequence will take the form of a drought, an obvious contrast to that which the Lord will provide to those who abide in His presence: "And it shall be, in that day, that living waters shall go out from Jerusalem" (Zech. 14:8).

ENDNOTES

[1] Since some Greek scholars believe John 7:53—8:11 was arbitrarily inserted into the account of Jesus' appearance at the Feast of Tabernacles, it is possible that Jesus made one other significant statement at that feast. Teaching in the Temple near the treasury (Jn. 8:20), Jesus spoke these words: "I am the light of the world; he that followeth me shall not walk in darkness, but shall have the light of life" (Jn. 8:12).

PART II
THE MINOR FEASTS
AND
FAST DAYS

A congregation observing Simchat Torah–
Rejoicing over the Law

8

SIMCHAT TORAH: REJOICING OVER THE LAW

All the world is dancing, singing,
    On this joyous holiday.
Hearts are merry, voices ringing,
    See how the Torah leads the way.
On! On! March along!
    All our voices join in song.
Hear the melody, lively, gay;
    This is Simchat Torah day.[1]

One of the happiest of all Jewish holidays is Simchat Torah. Second only to *Purim* in merriment, this delightful holiday needs but one word to describe it—joy. There is joy in the home. There is joy in the synagogue. There is joy throughout the entire Jewish community. The cause of this joy is found within the holiday's very name. *Simchat Torah* means *rejoicing over the law*. While the word *Torah* literally means *teaching*, *doctrine*, or *instruction*, it specifically refers to the five books of Moses, Genesis through Deuteronomy. Simchat Torah therefore has a noble purpose for such a jovial holiday—to celebrate the Bible, to be jubilant over the Word of God, to rejoice over the Torah!

Origin and Description of Simchat Torah

Characterized by singing, clapping hands, and dancing, Simchat Torah marks the annual completion of the public reading of the five books of Moses. Simchat Torah was not celebrated as a separate holiday in biblical days, nor was it observed in the days of the Talmudic rabbis. It was not until the ninth or tenth century that Simchat Torah became established as a distinct Jewish holiday.

Although the holiday itself is not biblical, the act of public Bible reading is. There are numerous examples of public Torah reading in the Old Testament (i.e., Josh. 8:34–35). By New Testament times the custom of reading the law of Moses every Sabbath was practiced widely (Acts 15:21). Later the Torah was read not only on the Sabbath but on Mondays and Thursdays as well.

When first practiced in the land of Israel, reading through the five books of Moses took three years. Eventually, due to the influence of the Jewish community in Babylon, each reading was made longer so that it could be completed within a one-year cycle. Modern Jewish communities still follow the one-year cycle. The Torah is divided into 54 readings with several portions combined on certain Sabbaths so that all 54 readings can be completed in one year.

Observance of Simchat Torah

Observed on the 23rd day of the Jewish month of Tishri (September–October), Simchat Torah immediately follows the Feast of Tabernacles. In Israel, however, the holiday is observed on the eighth day of Tabernacles, called Shemini Atzeret.

During the evening service in the synagogue, all the Torah scrolls are removed from the ark (a cabinet containing the scrolls) and joyfully carried around the auditorium seven times in a procession known as *hakkafot*. The children sing and carry flags decorated with apples and pictures of Torah scrolls.

Unique to the evening service of this holiday is the reading of a portion from the Torah. This is the only occasion during the year when the Torah is read at night. At the service the following morning, the same procession is repeated. After the hakkafot, all of the scrolls are returned to the ark, except three, which are used for the holiday's Torah readings. All of the adult males in the synagogue are called up to the bema (the platform where the Torah scroll is read) to share in this reading. At one point, all of the children are also summoned to the bema. An adult reads from the Torah as a large tallit (prayer shawl) is held above the children like a canopy.

The last reader of the first scroll receives the highly respected title of *Chatan Torah* (Bridegroom of the Torah). He is privileged to conclude the year's Torah reading cycle. Simchat Torah not only designates the completion of one Torah reading cycle, it also signals the beginning of another cycle, for on this day the reading of the second Torah scroll introduces the new cycle for the coming year. The honored reader of this portion is called *Chatan Bereshit* (Bridegroom of the Beginning). The final reader at the

Simchat Torah service reads from the third scroll a section of the day's portion from the Prophets.

After the service the Bridegroom of the Torah provides a sumptuous feast for the entire congregation. With the conclusion of Simchat Torah, there are no holidays on the Jewish calendar until the winter festival of *Hanukkah*.

Prophecy and Simchat Torah

With its post-biblical origin, Simchat Torah does not hold any prophetic implications, nor does the practice of public Torah reading deal with future events. Events prophesied to take place during the thousand-year earthly reign of the Messiah Jesus may however bear some resemblance to public Torah reading.

> *And many people shall go and say, Come ye, and let us go up to the mountain of the LORD, to the house of the God of Jacob; and he will teach us of his ways, and we will walk in his paths; for out of Zion shall go forth the law, and the word of the LORD from Jerusalem* (Isa. 2:3).

ENDNOTE

[1] "Yom Tov Lanu" from Harry Coopersmith, comp. and ed., *The New Jewish Song Book* (New York: Behrman House, Inc., 1965), 15–16.

The Hanukkah
Menorah and
Hanukkah Dreidel

9

HANUKKAH:
THE FESTIVAL OF LIGHTS

The year was 168 B.C. The place was a small town in ancient Israel. There the age-old battle between spiritual compromise and godly character was being waged.

The aged priest stood defiantly, his steely eyes firm in their resolve. "Be reasonable, old man," the captain urged, as his small band of soldiers nervously held back the crowd. The captain continued. "You know our orders. And you know the decree of his Excellency, King Antiochus Epiphanes [God Manifest]." "You mean Epimanes [Madman]," a wily onlooker called out.

The captain snarled, "Enough of this! Mattathias, you are a respected leader here in Modin. The people look up to you. This is your last chance to be a good example by presenting an offering to Zeus, our most high god. I want your final answer—now! Will you or will you not sacrifice this pig upon the altar?" All eyes turned toward the obstinate rebel. Surrounded by his five grown sons—John, Simeon, Judah (called Maccabeus), Eleazar, and Jonathan—Mattathias drew himself up, as if the challenge had somehow infused him with new strength.

The crowd held its breath as the old man took a step forward. Planting his feet and squaring his jaw, he was resolute in his reply: "Even if all the nations that live under the rule of the king obey him and have chosen to do his commandments, departing each one from the religion of his fathers," he declared, "yet I and my sons and my brothers will live by the covenant of our fathers. Far be it for us to desert the law and the ordinances. We will not obey the king's words by turning aside from our religion to the right hand or to the left."

"Very well," the captain hissed. "You will pay for your impertinence with your life." "No need to worry, captain," said a man strolling forward. "We Jews are not so inflexible that we cannot accommodate our Syrian friends and their Grecian ways. I will sacrifice your pig." The man took the knife, looked around as if for approval, then stepped toward the animal lying on the altar. The crowd was silent as a smug smile crossed the man's face.

Suddenly a howl of fury erupted from behind him. It was the voice of Mattathias. "No!" he screamed, racing toward the place of sacrifice. Pulling a sword from his tunic, Mattathias ran it through the horrified apostate. Seeing the courage of their father, his five sons unsheathed their swords and fell upon the captain and his troops. The battle was over in minutes.

Disgustedly, Mattathias demolished the unholy altar with its profane sacrifice. Then, standing over his defeated foes with sword in hand, he cried out to the timid bystanders, "If anyone be zealous for the laws of his country and for the worship of God, let him follow me!" And with that, Mattathias and his five sons scurried to the hills, beginning a prolonged season of guerrilla warfare against the evil forces of Syria and their king, Antiochus Epiphanes.

This story highlights an amazing period in Jewish history. The events that transpired after this episode resulted in one of Israel's most widely observed holidays, the winter festival of Hanukkah or the Festival of Lights.

Origin and Description of Hanukkah

The holiday of Hanukkah (lit., *Dedication*) is not a God-given feast day. It is a man-made festival commemorating a great military and spiritual achievement by the Jewish people during one of the darkest periods in their history.

The event took place during the 400 years between the Old and New Testaments, during which the nation of Israel underwent dramatic changes. The greatest change occurred when a young Macedonian general, Alexander the Great, conquered most of the then-known world by the time he was 33 years of age. The subjugated territory included the land of Israel.

Alexander was a ruthless soldier, but he was also a wise diplomat. He understood that the best way to insure a united kingdom was to create a universal culture that spoke the same language, learned the same philosophies, experienced the same pleasures, and worshiped the same gods. Thus, the influence and permeation of Greek culture and lifestyle were the most powerful weapons Alexander had at his disposal, and he used them thoroughly. This Hellenization of the world also affected, of course, the nation of Israel. It was in this complete cultural change of identity that the people of God found their biggest challenge and threat.

After Alexander died at the age of 33, as a result of a life of debauchery, his kingdom was divided among four of his leading generals. Two of the resulting dynasties were known as the Ptolemaic and Seleucid empires. The Ptolemaic empire was headquartered in Alexandria, Egypt, while the Seleucid empire was headquartered in Antioch, Syria. Located in the middle of these two conflicting kingdoms, Israel received the brunt of their mutual animosities. The most difficult period for Israel came when the Seleucid ruler Antiochus IV (or Epiphanes [God Manifest], as he dubbed himself) came to power. In the year 168 B.C., Antiochus embarked on an expedition to Egypt to subdue his long-time rivals. He met with some success in his military efforts; however, just as he was ready to apply the *coup de grace*, a power from the West interrupted his plans. Rome demanded that he cease his military campaign against Egypt and return to Syria. If he did not, he and his forces would suffer the wrath of Rome in all of its fury.

Antiochus had no choice and reluctantly withdrew from Egypt. On his return to Syria, he found a way to vent his disappointment and anger. Passing through Israel, he decided on a series of measures that he thought would once and for all eliminate his troubles with the Jewish people. Reaffirming Alexander's dream of making a one-world people through a one-world culture, Antiochus decreed that the Jews would have to change. From that point on, the Jewish people were forbidden under penalty of death from circumcising their newborn boys, celebrating the Jewish festivals, keeping the Sabbath, offering the daily sacrifices, and reading or having in their possession a copy of the Torah. Coupled with that, all Jewish people in every locale were required to erect altars dedicated to Zeus, the chief god of the Greeks. On these altars they were forced to sacrifice swine—obviously an unclean and abhorrent animal to the Jews—and pay homage to Greek deities. To accentuate his point, Antiochus marched into the Jewish Temple in Jerusalem, stole its ornaments, set up an image of Zeus on the bronze altar, and there sacrificed a pig in the sight of everyone. The date was the 25th day of the month Kislev, 168 B.C.

This turn of events stunned the Jewish populace. They were forced to show their allegiance one way or the other. There could be no middle ground in this situation. They would either follow the Lord and

keep His ways, paying the penalty with their lives, or cave in to the
pressure and adopt the Grecian customs. It was a difficult decision.
Many Israelites chose to compromise. When weighing the
options, they though it would be better to be alive and apostate
than to be dead and orthodox. Those who chose to accept the
Greek culture often took Greek names. They studied Greek literature and philosophy. They even participated in or attended the
new Greek gymnasium in Jerusalem, where athletes participated
in sporting events completely naked before the audience. Some
Jewish athletes went so far as to have special operations to hide
their circumcision. Those who, to one degree or another, were
influenced by Greek culture became known as Hellenized Jews.
The Hellenized Jews were not looked upon favorably by the Jews
who strove to keep the traditional customs and laws. The ill will
between these two groups could be seen even in the early church.
Acts 6:1 records the account of the widows of Hellenized Jews
who were being overlooked by the Hebraic Jews in the daily serving of food. A small matter perhaps, but one that sheds light on
the tension and prejudice that existed between the two factions.
Those who did not give in to the decrees of Antiochus but kept
their strong Jewish faith were brutally tortured and murdered.
Antiochus was true to his word in that regard. Thousands perished under his wicked schemes.

Shortly after Antiochus issued his decrees and defiled the
Temple, a contingent of his enforcers came upon the small town
of Modin, just northwest of Jerusalem, where Mattathias and his
five sons lived. Following the events at the altar to Zeus that
were described earlier in this chapter, Mattathias fled to the hills
with his sons and anyone else who chose to follow. During the
next year, Mattathias attacked Syrian outposts, destroyed foreign
idols and their altars, and had infant boys circumcised. At the end
of that year Mattathias passed away, but not before entrusting his

son, Judah Maccabeus, with the army. It was a wise choice.

It was not long before Judah and his men were tested in battle by the Syrians. Facing overwhelming odds, at times confronting enemy armies 13 times the size of theirs, Judah and his men became seasoned warriors. Following one of their victories, Judah informed his troops that it was time to go up to Jerusalem. The sight that met their eyes upon entering the Temple Mount reduced many to tears. The doors of the Temple were burnt. The holy curtains had been torn down. Weeds were sprouting through the Temple pavement, which had been vacant and neglected for many years. The altar of burnt offering was defiled with an idol of Zeus and the remains of sacrificed pigs. It was a scene almost too difficult to bear.

Despite the grievous circumstances, Judah the Maccabee rallied his troops. He commissioned them in the holy task of cleansing the Temple and consecrating it again to God. The following days were filled with activity. They purged the Temple area. They constructed a new Temple lampstand, a new table of showbread, a new altar of incense, new curtains, and new doors. They also tore down the old altar of burnt offering and replaced it with a new one fashioned of uncut stones.

At last the task was complete. On the 25th day of Kislev, 165 B.C., exactly three years to the day from when it was desecrated by Antiochus and his troops, Judah and the people of Israel dedicated the cleansed Temple. It was dedicated not to Zeus or Apollo but to the ancient and ever-living God of Abraham, Isaac, and Jacob. It was a solemn hour. It was also a time of rejoicing. The celebration lasted for eight days and featured music, feasting, worshiping, and praising God. Judah then decreed that such a festival should be instituted and observed every year, lasting for eight days and memorializing the "restoration of their Temple worship."[1] Thus was established what became known as the Feast of Dedication or Hanukkah.

There has been some debate as to why the Maccabees chose to fix the duration of Hanukkah at eight days. According to one legend, when the Maccabees came upon the Temple, they found only one cruse of consecrated oil still intact with which to light the eternal flame of the menorah. The legend goes on to say that the oil miraculously lasted for eight days, allowing enough time for more consecrated oil to be produced. This story is not found in any of the earliest accounts of these events. The miracle of the oil is therefore probably fictitious and was added to the Hanukkah story to help perpetuate the holiday's observance. This was not needed, however, because the real miracle of the story is how God protected His people and delivered them from their evil oppressors. Nevertheless, the legendary miracle of the oil is the reason most Jewish people give today for why Hanukkah is celebrated for eight days.

Observance of Hanukkah

Beginning on the 25th day of the Jewish month of Kislev (November–December), Hanukkah is observed for eight days. Although originally a minor festival, over the years it has become one of the two festivals most widely observed by American Jews, Passover being the other. Hanukkah is a joyous time with happy meals, family gatherings, and playful activities for the children. Work is allowed during the Hanukkah season, but it is not encouraged.

Hanukkah begins in the home with the customary lighting of the holiday candles. The candelabra that is used is unique to Hanukkah. The Hanukkah menorah or *hanukkiyah* has nine candlesticks. One candle is added each evening in memory of the eight days that the oil purportedly lasted in the time of the Maccabees. The ninth candle, called the *shammash* (servant), is used to light the other eight. The menorah is usually placed near a front window so that its lighting may serve as a testimony to the

miracle that occurred long ago.   After lighting the Hanukkah
menorah, the family often sings songs.   One traditional hymn
entitled *Maoz Tzur* speaks of God's power to deliver.

> Rock of ages, let our song
>   Praise Your saving power;
> You amidst the raging throng
>   Were our sheltering tower.
> Furious they assailed us,
>   But Your help availed us;
> And your word broke their sword
>   When our own strength failed us.

Special foods are eaten at Hanukkah meals.   Oil-fried dishes,
such as crispy potato pancakes (called *latkes*) eaten with apple-
sauce or other toppings are common on Hanukkah in memory of
the Maccabean *miracle* oil.   In Israel, doughnuts are prevalent.

Later in the evening, the moment the children anxiously await
finally arrives.   Hanukkah gifts are exchanged.   Some parents
give their children all of their gifts on the first night, while others
spread them out over the eight-day period.   Children also often
receive Hanukkah *gelt* (money) in the form of coins made of
chocolate or actual coins.

Along with the gifts, Jewish children also enjoy playing a traditional game called Spin the *Dreidel*.   The dreidel is a four-sided top.
The children spin the top to see who wins the game.   Candy, coins,
or other items are used for stakes.   On each of the four sides of the
top is a Hebrew letter.   The four letters combine to form an acrostic that stands for "A great miracle happened there."   Once the State
of Israel came into being, one letter was changed on Israeli dreidels
so that the acrostic reads, "A great miracle happened here."

In Israel Hanukkah also is celebrated with torch relay races
from the ancient town of Modin up to the city of Jerusalem.
Large Hanukkah menorahs are placed atop public buildings.

Handel's oratorio, *Judas Maccabaeus*, is occasionally performed.

There can be no doubt that the manner in which Hanukkah is observed today has been highly influenced by the holiday of Christmas. Both holidays occur around the same time of the year. Both holidays feature warm family gatherings full of happiness and good cheer. Yet it has been difficult for the Jewish minority living in the midst of an overwhelmingly Gentile majority to retain a distinct, Jewish Hanukkah identity at this season. Surrounded by Christmas carols, jolly Santas, and Bethlehem scenes, it has been hard not to incorporate just a little bit of the "Christmas spirit" into the Hanukkah celebration. Some Jewish families even bring a Christmas tree or *Hanukkah bush* into their homes, which they decorate as any non-Jewish family would. Other Jewish families try to resist the temptation. As one Jewish author put it, "Appreciation does not mean appropriation. Because appropriation leads to confusion, loss of identity, and, ultimately, assimilation. And assimilation is what the Maccabees and generations of Jews after them fought so hard to prevent. To appropriate Christmas into our homes would give posthumous victory to Antiochus. Christmas does not belong in a Jewish home—period."[2]

This author's point is well taken. It would be an accurate statement and a legitimate concern if not for one detail. The reason for Christmas is Christ. If Jesus is the Messiah, as He claimed to be, then incorporating a celebration of His birth into the Hanukkah festivities would not be a denial of the Jewish faith but, rather, a culminating affirmation of it. It would be an "assimilation" into the truth, which is something not to avoid but to embrace.

Prophecy and Hanukkah

Being a man-made holiday, the festival of Hanukkah has no prophetic import. The events surrounding the festival of Hanukkah, however, were predicted in Scripture long before they happened.   In Daniel 11:21–35, the exploits of Antiochus Epiphanes and his ensuing campaign to wipe out biblical Judaism are outlined in great detail.

An interesting aspect of this text is found in Daniel 11:36, where the narrative still seems to be referring to Antiochus, and yet the description does not match any recorded historical events. Many prophetic scholars therefore think that Daniel 11:36–45 describes another individual commonly referred to as the Antichrist, who is yet to appear on the scene but is typified in the person of Antiochus Epiphanes.

As Antiochus beguiled Israel into false security[3], so too will the Antichrist (Dan. 9:27).   As Antiochus thought himself to be God, so too will the Antichrist (Dan. 11:36-37; 2 Th. 2:4).   As Antiochus persecuted the Jewish people (Dan. 11:33), so too will the Antichrist (Dan. 12:1; Mt. 24:21).   As Antiochus abolished the practice of Judaism and set up the abomination of desolation (Dan. 11:31), so too will the Antichrist (Dan. 9:27; Mt. 24:15).   Thus we see that although the holiday of Hanukkah is not emphasized in Scripture, the events that led up to the creation of the holiday are a part of Scripture.   More so, they serve as a foreshadowing of another turbulent time in Israel's history that is yet to come.

One passage in the Bible, John 10:22, does specifically mention the holiday of Hanukkah.   The text reads, "And it was at Jerusalem the feast of the dedication [Hanukkah], and it was winter."   On this occasion Jesus made a most startling declaration. While Jesus was walking in the Temple, the people demanded that He tell them plainly whether or not He was the Messiah. Jesus replied that He had already told them that He was the Messiah and that His miracles confirmed His messianic credentials.   The problem was not His messianic claims.   The problem was that some of the people did not believe Him.   Some, however, did believe.   These people He referred to as His sheep, to whom He gave eternal life and eternal security. No one could pluck them out of His hand, Jesus asserted, and no one could pluck them out of His heavenly Father's hand.

Then, stunning the crowd, Jesus made a remarkable statement. He proclaimed, "I and my Father are one" (Jn. 10:30). In this statement, Jesus was declaring clearly that He and God the Father were of the same nature. He was saying that he was equal to God in all respects. The *Shema* (Dt. 6:4), the primary Jewish declaration of faith, proclaims that the Lord, Israel's God, is one Lord: "Hear, O Israel: The LORD our God is one LORD." The word for "one" in this verse, however, is often used in Scripture to describe a plurality in unity (i.e., Gen. 2:24). Therefore, here and in other Old Testament passages (i.e., Isa. 48:12–16), there is a hint of the triune nature of God that is more fully revealed in the New Testament. Jesus was simply affirming this truth. There is only one God, but He exists in a plurality of being. Jesus is part of that plurality. In simple terms, He, Jesus Christ, was pronouncing, "I am God in the flesh."

The multitude that heard Him was taken aback. They understood exactly what Jesus meant. This can be seen by their reaction to His statement. They picked up stones to stone Him. "Many good works have I shown you from my Father; for which of those works do ye stone me?" (Jn. 10:32), Jesus asked. "For a good work we stone thee not," they answered, "but for blasphemy; and because that thou, being a man, makest thyself God" (Jn. 10:33). The Jewish people considered it blasphemy for anyone to declare Himself to be God. They remembered how, almost two hundred years before, another man—Antiochus IV—made a similar claim when he chose to call himself Epiphanes (God Manifest). And on this occasion, during Hanukkah of all times, they were not about to let that same mistake happen again.

It was not an accident that Jesus chose Hanukkah as the time to proclaim His deity. He knew exactly what He was doing. Jesus answered the insulted throng by pointing to their own Scriptures. In Psalm 82:6 there is a precedent for calling someone the son of God. The psalmist wrote, "I have said, Ye are gods; and all of you are children of the Most High." This must have been a familiar psalm to the people because it was sung by the Levites every Tuesday in the Temple. If even the psalmist, under the inspiration of the Holy Spirit, called human beings "gods," Jesus asked, why then was He being accused of blasphemy when He had proven by His life and ministry that he was no mere human being? "If I do not the works of my Father, believe me not. But if I do, though ye believe not me, believe the works, that ye may know, and believe, that the Father is in me, and I in him" (Jn. 10:37–38).

Jesus' final word to the people during Hanukkah was directed as a challenge. In effect He was saying, "You may not like what I say, but I back it up with my life. Take a look at what I have done. Inspect it, examine it, dissect it if you wish. But you will not be able to honestly get around the fact that I am who I say I am—the Son of God, the Messiah."

This statement did nothing to dissuade the offended crowd. They attempted once more to apprehend Jesus, but He escaped from their midst (Jn. 10:39). Jesus made His point nonetheless. He was not a mere scholar, a simple rabbi, or just a good teacher of the law. He made it clear that He was different from all men. He was distinct. He was man, but He was also God.

How do we know this for sure? The answer is found in the empty tomb. The greatest reason for believing that Jesus was and is who He claimed to be is that He was not in the tomb. He had and is risen. As the Scripture says, "I will declare the decree: The LORD hath said unto me, Thou art my Son; this day have I begotten thee" (Ps. 2:7). To which day was the psalmist referring? The Book of Acts reveals the answer. "And we declare unto you glad tidings, how the promise which was made unto the fathers, God hath fulfilled the same unto us their children, in that he hath raised up Jesus again; as it is also written in the second psalm, Thou art my Son, this day have I begotten thee" (Acts 13:32–33).

On the day of Jesus' resurrection from the dead, God trumpeted the news to all of mankind: "This is my Son. This is my proof." As the Apostle Paul explained, "Concerning his Son, Jesus Christ our Lord, who was made of the seed of David according to the flesh, And declared to be the Son of God with power, according to the spirit of holiness, by the resurrection from the dead" (Rom. 1:3–4).

It is on this point, then, that the appearance of Jesus at the Feast of Dedication takes on meaning. Antiochus IV claimed to be God. So did Jesus. The difference between the two is that Antiochus IV was and is dead. Jesus Christ, however, is very much alive. Which one, therefore, was telling the truth?

As a final note to Hanukkah's relationship to prophecy, it is not known if the holiday will be a part of the future Millennial Kingdom when Jesus reigns on the earth. Scripture is silent on the matter. Being a man-made festival, however, it is unlikely that it will be a part of the kingdom holidays.

ENDNOTES

[1] William Whiston, trans., *Josephus* (Grand Rapids: Kregel Publications, 1960), *Antiquities of the Jews*, 12.7.7.

[2] Ron Wolfson, *The Art of Jewish Living: Hanukkah* (New York: The Federation of Jewish Men's Clubs, 1990), 173.

[3] Josephus, *Antiquities*, 12.5.4: ". . .the king [Antiochus] came up to Jerusalem, and, pretending peace, he got possession of the city by treachery."

The Purim Gregger and
a basket of Hamantaschen

10

PURIM: JOYOUSLY CELEBRATING THE FAITHFULNESS OF GOD

Imagine that you are watching a huge celebration take place. There are throngs of people milling about, young and old alike. Everyone is having a wonderful time. But you are unaware of the purpose of the occasion. Nearby you see a large group of people twirling noisemakers, making as much commotion as they possibly can. Some are imbibing alcohol quite heavily. You conclude that it must be New Year's Eve. But your conclusion would be wrong.

Then you see other people masquerading around in all sorts of costumes. You spy a clown, someone with a false beard, a king, and a lovely queen. You then assume the occasion must be Halloween. But you would again be mistaken. Suddenly you see a parade coming down the street. There are floats and marching bands. It must be Thanksgiving, you surmise. Sorry, wrong again.

Finally you observe friends and family exchanging food baskets and other people giving monetary gifts to the poor. "Aha!"

you exclaim. "It's Christmas!" But once more your conclusion is wrong. Give up? The celebration you would be watching is the holiday of Purim, the happiest day on the Jewish calendar.

Origin and Description of Purim

The story of Purim is found in the Book of Esther. Apart from the name of the king, neither the main characters of the account nor the holiday itself are mentioned anywhere else in the Bible. The holiday of Purim is a man-made festival that originated out of the decrees of Mordecai and Queen Esther (Est. 9:29–32). Although Purim was founded in biblical times, it is not a holiday commanded by God, as are the holy convocations mentioned in Leviticus 23. The events surrounding the story took place roughly between 483 to 471 B.C. The narrative is well known.

As the tale begins, King Ahasuerus is the king of Persia. In the third year of his reign, Ahasuerus decided to celebrate his sovereignty by giving a lavish party that would last more than six months. After a considerable amount of drinking, the king decided to display his most prized possession, his wife Vashti. Ahasuerus commanded her to come and appear before his royal guests. Jewish tradition says that he instructed her to appear nude. Queen Vashti rejected the idea of exposing herself so immodestly and spurned her husband's order.

King Ahasuerus was incensed and retreated to his counselors for advice. The counselors advised him to depose Vashti as queen, send out an edict commanding all wives in the empire to obey their husbands, and institute a search for the most beautiful maiden in the empire, who would then take Vashti's place. King Ahasuerus listened to his counselors and did as they suggested. Vashti lost her crown (Jewish tradition says that she was executed), and a search began for the next queen.

Meanwhile, King Ahasuerus sent his armies to do battle

against an old nemesis, Greece. But in 480 B.C., at the naval battle of Salamis, Ahasuerus, otherwise known to historians as Xerxes, was soundly defeated. The beauty search continued, nevertheless, and a young Jewish girl was selected to participate in the contest. Her name was *Hadassah* (meaning *Myrtle*), but she later came to be known by her Persian name, Esther.

Esther was an orphan who was raised by her cousin Mordecai. Mordecai was of the tribe of Benjamin and possibly from the house of Saul (Est. 2:5). When Esther was taken to the palace, Mordecai instructed her not to reveal her ethnic background, most likely out of concern that it would be held against her. The Jews were a subservient people to the Persians at that time and therefore would have been considered members of a lower class, an order of commoners and peasants. Eventually the search came to an end and, in God's sovereignty, Esther was chosen to be the new queen of Persia. Mordecai was also given an official position sitting at the king's gate.

One day Mordecai uncovered an assassination plot against the king. Political intrigue and assassinations were not uncommon in the ancient world. In fact, King Ahasuerus did eventually perish at the hands of assassins. In this instance, however, the conspirators were revealed. Through Esther, Mordecai informed the king of the plot, and the perpetrators were executed. A record of Mordecai's assistance was duly noted, but he received no reward.

Around that time, the king promoted a man who eventually became one of Israel's all-time worst enemies. His name was Haman, and he is described as the "son of Hammedatha, the Agagite" (Est. 3:1).

Haman's lineage is significant to the story of Purim. He was a descendant of Agag, who was king of the Amalekites in the days of Saul and Samuel. Saul defeated Agag but disobeyed the Lord by allowing him to live. The Prophet Samuel rebuked King Saul for his disobedience then "hewed Agag in pieces before the LORD" (1 Sam. 15:33).

Being an Amalekite, Agag was part of the group of people who were long-term enemies of Israel. Because of their treatment of the children of Israel in the days of Moses, God declared war on Amalek "from generation to generation" (Ex. 17:16). In Jewish teaching, Amalek is seen as the epitome of anti-Semitism. As one Jewish author wrote, "The very essence of Amalek is hatred of Israel; without prospect of self gain; hatred without cause or motive; hatred for the sake of hatred alone; a hatred which never ceases."[1]

Haman therefore had a heritage of enmity toward the Jewish people. As the story of Esther unfolds, we can see how Haman exhibited his own type of evil hatred.

Haman was elevated by King Ahasuerus to a position above everyone else in the kingdom but the king himself. Everyone who saw Haman was required to bow down and pay him homage. Everyone obeyed the king's command except one man—Mordecai. He stubbornly refused to bow before Haman, perhaps because Haman was an Amalekite or perhaps because, as a Jew, Mordecai did not want to appear to be worshiping anyone other than God. Whatever the reason, Mordecai's behavior infuriated Haman.

Having learned that Mordecai was a Jew, Haman determined to kill him. But not satisfied with the murder of one single Jew, he plotted to wipe out all of the Jewish people in the empire. The Bible records that during the first month of the Jewish calendar, Nisan, Haman sat down and *rolled the dice*, so to speak, on the Jewish people. Through the use of some sort of tokens called "lots," Haman tried to determine the right date to seal Israel's fate. Each lot was known as a "Pur," from which the name of the holiday was eventually derived. Most likely using Persian astrology to project a good date, Haman decided upon the 13th day of the month Adar (the 12th month on the Jewish calendar) as the luckiest time for carrying out his diabolical scheme.

Haman then laid out his request before the king. Depicting the mind-set of every anti-Semite that has ever lived, Haman pointed out that there was "a certain people" different from the rest of the king's subjects. These people were so odd, he convinced the king, that they deserved to die. Haman was even willing to cover the cost of this genocidal operation. The king irresponsibly gave Haman permission to implement his plan, and shortly thereafter Haman issued the edict. The declaration advised of the forthcoming mandated destruction of all Jewish people in the empire. The official document specified the date the event was to occur, and it also stated that everyone who participated in the killing could help themselves to the spoils left behind. The edict was final. It was a Persian law that once the king had issued a decree, it could not be rescinded. Satisfied, Haman smugly sat down to eat and drink with the king, anticipating his revenge upon Mordecai and all the Jews.

When the news of their impending destruction reached the Jewish community, they were devastated. Throughout the empire the Jewish people mourned, fasted, and wept. All hope seemed lost. Even Mordecai walked around in sackcloth and ashes, distraught over what was about to happen to him and his people. Queen Esther, upon hearing of the sad condition of her beloved foster parent, sent gifts to cheer him. But Mordecai sent word to her describing the evil plot of wicked Haman. He implored Esther to act on behalf of her people and plead for their lives before the king.

Esther responded by informing Mordecai that anyone who came uninvited into the king's chambers could suffer immediate death. History records that there were guards stationed near the king at all times. Each guard bore an ax that he would bring down upon anyone who approached the king without an invitation. The only way a person was spared was if the king stretched out his golden scepter, indicating his acceptance of his or her unannounced entrance.

This did not dissuade Mordecai, however. He replied to Queen Esther that she should nevertheless go before the king and incur the risk. Courageously, Esther followed his instructions. She asked only that the Jewish community pray and fast on her behalf for three days. She then would go before the king. She solemnly declared, "And if I perish, I perish" (Est. 4:16).

Archaeologists have unearthed the winter palace of King Ahasuerus in the city of Shushan, or Susa. The royal palace (Est. 5:1-2) had three courts. "The walls were of sun-dried brick covered with whitewash on the inside, and the paving was coated throughout with polished red ochre."[2] It was through these royal halls that Esther must have walked three days later, not knowing if her life would shortly be taken from her. But as the king beheld Esther standing in the court, his heart was moved with her beauty. He stretched out his golden scepter, receiving her into his presence. When the king asked her request, Queen Esther invited him and Haman to a banquet she planned to give in their honor. Quickly the arrangements were made, and the banquet was held. During the party Esther made a second request. She asked the king and Haman to attend another banquet on the following day.

As Haman returned home, his proud heart was lifted up. He rehearsed all of his glories and achievements to his family and friends, particularly his status as the sole guest at the king and queen's banquet. But none of this satisfied Haman because Mordecai the Jew still refused to pay him the respect he demanded. Haman's wife then offered a suggestion. Why not hang Mordecai on a gallows? In fact, why not make it a particularly visible gallows, about 50 cubits (approximately 75 feet) high? The thought pleased Haman, and he commanded that work on the gallows begin immediately. He decided to petition the king the next morning for Mordecai's life, after which he would go rejoicing to Queen Esther's banquet.

Unknown to Haman, however, the king was struck with insomnia that very night. Seeking relief, he had the chronicles of his kingdom read aloud to him. Hearing the account of Mordecai's saving his life, Ahasuerus asked what had been done for Mordecai to reward him for his loyalty. The answer was nothing. At that very moment, Haman arrived to ask for Mordecai's execution. Before he could speak, the king asked him what he thought should be done for a man whom the king desired to honor. Bloated with pride and conceit, Haman assumed that the king was referring to him. Thinking this an opportune time to acquire glory for himself, Haman laid out an elaborate honorarium, not the least part of which was having a prince lead the dignitary through the streets of the capital on horseback heralding his greatness.

Haman was pleased when the king agreed to his suggested laurels, but he must have been stunned when the king bestowed those laurels on Mordecai. Worse than that, the herald leading Mordecai through the streets of the capital would be Haman himself. Chagrined and humiliated, Haman obeyed the king's command and finally gave Mordecai the honor he was due.

After glorifying Mordecai, Haman hurried home and poured out his troubles to his family and friends. They were not very comforting, however. They told him that if Mordecai was a Jew, he would not prevail against him but would cause his own ruin. Just then messengers came and whisked Haman away to the queen's banquet. Then Esther finally revealed her motives for appearing before the king. She wanted to plead for the lives of her countrymen who were about to be wiped out. Shocked, the king asked who would do such a thing. Dramatically, the queen revealed the truth. "The adversary and enemy," she said, "is this wicked Haman" (Est. 7:6).

The king, realizing that he had been tricked by his top cabinet member, left the room in anger and retreated to the palace garden.

Meanwhile, Haman desperately sought the queen's mercy. Not thinking of appearances, Haman flung himself on Esther's bed and begged for his life. Suddenly the king returned and saw Haman in this compromising position. Assuming that he was attempting to molest his wife, the king asked what should be done to such a vile person. One of his chamberlains suggested that Haman be hung on the same gallows that he had prepared for Mordecai. And so it was done. The king then installed Mordecai in the place of Haman.

But the Jews still faced certain death. Esther appeared before the king again, and again he extended the golden scepter of acceptance to her. Begging for the lives of her people, Esther pleaded with the king to do something about the destructive edict that Haman had formulated. The problem was that under Persian law it could not be rescinded. Therefore, King Ahasuerus instructed Esther and Mordecai to prepare their own edict, giving the Jews throughout the kingdom permission to defend themselves against anyone who attacked them on the 13th of Adar. The king also gave the Jewish community permission to take as spoils any of their defeated enemies' possessions.

When the new decree was announced, the Jewish people rejoiced. Their darkness had turned to light. Seeing that the Jewish people were now in a position of blessing, many of the Persian people converted to Judaism out of fear. Then came the fateful day—the 13th of Adar. The Jewish people were ready for their attackers. Fear of Mordecai had already permeated the ranks of the anti-Semites, and they were afraid that they would be thoroughly defeated, which they were. The Jewish community's victory celebration lasted for two days in the winter capital of Susa and included the hanging of Haman's ten sons. Interestingly, the biblical text records three times that even though the Jewish people successfully defended themselves, they did not take any spoils.

This indicates that their actions were not motivated by greed.

Mordecai and Esther prescribed that the Jewish people should keep the 14th and 15th of Adar as an annual celebration, through their generations, to commemorate their great deliverance.

Observance of Purim

Purim is a minor holiday on the Jewish calendar. The majority of modern Jewish people do not observe it, and those who do, do so primarily for the sake of their children. Purim is observed on the 14th of Adar (February-March). In Jerusalem it is also celebrated on the 15th, as it was in the ancient city of Susa. When the Jewish calendar has a leap year, a second month of Adar is added, and the observance of Purim is postponed until this second date.

The central activity on Purim is reading the Book of Esther. A *Megillah* or scroll is taken out and folded like a letter. The entire story of Esther is read from this scroll. This is done in the synagogue. Based on the command to "blot out the remembrance of Amalek from under heaven" (Dt. 25:19), an unusual custom developed and has long been practiced. As the Megillah is read, every time the name of Haman is mentioned the listeners boo, hiss, stomp their feet, whistle, pound plastic, air-filled hammers, or spin noisemakers called *greggers*. The idea is to make so much noise that the memory of Haman, an Amalekite, is blotted out from under heaven.

In the home, a special holiday meal is eaten in the afternoon. This meal must be plentiful and festive. *Hamantashen*, a three-corner pastry filled with poppy seeds, prunes, or other fruits and said to resemble Haman's hat, is a holiday favorite. It is also customary to give small baskets full of cooked foods to friends on Purim. And a few coins are handed out to the poor.

The underlying theme of every Purim activity is fun. It is the most joyous of all Jewish holidays. Happiness and good cheer are the highlights of this day's celebration. There is singing, dancing, and an almost carnival-like atmosphere. Children and even some adults dress in costumes. Purim plays are presented. People who are usually held in high esteem, such as rabbis, are good-naturedly parodied and made the brunt of jokes. In Israel, there are Purim parades with large floats and marching bands.

The most controversial aspect of the Purim celebration is found in the Talmud, which states, "It is the duty of a man to mellow himself [with wine] on Purim until he cannot tell the difference between 'cursed be Haman' and 'blessed be Mordecai.' "[3] The phrases "cursed be Haman" and "blessed be Mordecai" are found in a prayer that follows the reading of the Megillah. The idea is that on Purim it is permissible to drink alcoholic beverages to such a degree that people find it difficult to distinguish between the cursing and blessing of this prayer. Some people in the Jewish community do imbibe a great deal of alcohol on Purim. Others feel that getting drunk on Purim is excessive. They interpret the Talmudic injunction to simply mean lie down to rest from the exhaustion of the celebration. Unfortunately, however, heavy drinking has become a part of the fun-making traditions of Purim.

Prophecy and Purim

Being a man-made holiday, there is no direct correlation between Purim and biblical prophecy. Nor is there any clear typology between this festival and the person of Jesus the Messiah.

Jewish tradition however believes that Purim will be one of the few Jewish festivals to continue in the days of the Messiah and his kingdom. At that time, Purim will serve as a memorial. It will be a remembrance of the beginning of the annihilation of Amalek during the days of Mordecai and Esther and their final annihilation at the coming of the Messiah.

ENDNOTES

[1] Eliyahu Kitov, *The Book of Our Heritage*, trans. Nathan Bulman, rev. ed., 3 vols. (Jerusalem: Feldheim Publishers, 1978), 2:34.

[2] Jack Finegan, *Light From the Ancient Past: The Archaeological Background of Judaism and Christianity*, 2 vols. (Princeton: Princeton University Press, 1959), 1:243.

[3] *The Babylonian Talmud*, trans. under the editorship of Rabbi Dr. I. Epstein, et al., 18 vols. (London: The Soncino Press, 1938), Megillah 7b.

The Street of the Righteous Gentiles
Yad Vashem, Jerusalem

11

YOM HA-SHO'AH: THE HOLOCAUST REMEMBRANCE DAY

Never shall I forget that night, the first night in camp, which has turned my life into one long night, seven times cursed and seven times sealed. Never shall I forget that smoke. Never shall I forget the little faces of the children, whose bodies I saw turned into wreaths of smoke beneath a silent blue sky.

Never shall I forget those flames which consumed my faith forever.

Never shall I forget that nocturnal silence which deprived me, for all eternity, of the desire to live. Never shall I forget those moments which murdered my God and my soul and turned my dreams to dust. Never shall I forget these things, even if I am condemned to live as long as God Himself. Never.[1]

Describing the first night in Auschwitz, these are the haunting words of Elie Wiesel, a survivor of what he called "the ante-chamber of Hell." Auschwitz, infamous monolith of Nazi cruelty, is the place where more than two million people were murdered between 1941 and 1944. Today it stands as a silent memorial of one of mankind's darkest hours—the Holocaust of World War II.

To provide a legacy for those who follow, as well as to show reverence for those who perished, a solemn anniversary was added to the list of Jewish commemorative days. *Yom ha-Sho'ah* (lit., *Day of the Holocaust*) was established with one purpose in mind: to never forget.

Origin and Description of Yom ha-Sho'ah

In 1933 Adolf Hitler was appointed Chancellor of Germany. For the next 12 years the devastating consequences of that appointment were felt around the world. The end result was the death of 45 million people. Hitler's megalomania resulted in a conflict that involved people worldwide, but none were affected by his vitriolic attacks more than the Jewish people.

Hitler considered the Jewish people to be the paramount threat to human advancement and, specifically, to Aryan racial purity. His policies as *Fuhrer* (*Leader*) reflected this belief. Jewish people were first defined (anyone with at least one Jewish grandparent) and then singled out for various forms of discrimination and persecution. As Raul Hilberg put it, "More and more was taken from the Jews; less and less was given in return. The Jews were deprived of their professions, their enterprises, their financial reserves, their wages, their claims upon food and shelter, and, finally, their last personal belongings, down to underwear, gold teeth, and women's hair."[2]

What became known as the "Final Solution" to the "Jewish

problem" was efficiently administered through confinement, isolation, starvation, and systematic extermination. Fifteen major concentration camps were set up by the Nazis. Four more were established solely as death camps. Arriving prisoners were stripped, shaved, lethally gassed, and cremated in specially built crematoriums or in open pits. By the end of the war in 1945, more than one-third of worldwide Jewry had been destroyed by the evil machinations of the Third Reich. Six million Jews had been mercilessly killed, their bodies turned to ashes or left lying in unmarked mass graves.

To remember the fathers, mothers, sisters, brothers, spouses, children—everyone who had perished—on April 12, 1951, the Israeli Knesset established "The Holocaust and Ghetto Uprising Remembrance Day—a day of perpetual remembrance for the House of Israel,"[3] later shortened to Yom ha-Sho'ah.

Observance of Yom ha-Sho'ah

Most likely due to its recent establishment, there is general disagreement as to how Yom ha-Sho'ah is to be observed, if at all. Even the day of its observance is not agreed upon. In the State of Israel Yom ha-Sho'ah is observed on the 27th day of the month Nisan (March-April). This date was chosen because it falls between the date of the Warsaw Ghetto uprising (Nisan 14) in 1943 and that of Israel's War of Independence Remembrance Day (Iyyar 4). Jews outside of Israel usually observe Yom ha-Sho'ah on April 19, which coincides with the Gregorian date of the Warsaw Ghetto uprising.

Ceremonies of Yom ha-Sho'ah are also widely divergent. In Israel the national Holocaust memorial center, *Yad Vashem*, strives to bring an awareness of the day and its meaning through various activities and functions. Wreaths are laid and solemn music is played, while prayers and words of tribute are said over the eternal flame that burns in memory of the Holocaust victims. All places of entertainment are closed on the eve of Yom ha-Sho'ah. During the day a two-minute-long siren blast throughout the country calls everyone to stop what they are doing and stand completely still. After this painful reminder, activities resume and life goes on.

Religious ceremonies have been established in both the Reform and Conservative branches of Judaism, with the addition of appropriate prayers and readings from their prayer books. The ultra-Orthodox, however, do not observe Yom ha-Sho'ah. With so many other fast days already commemorating Jewish tragedies, they do not feel that a special day for the Holocaust is needed.

In the home, there are often candle-lighting ceremonies and prayers. The events of the Holocaust are discussed. Fasting, or at least sparse eating, is encouraged to identify with those who starved to death in the concentration camps. Instead of fasting from food, some feel they should fast from speaking to create a more contemplative and reflective mood on this somber day. Monetary gifts to Holocaust memorials are also customary.

Prophecy and Yom ha-Sho'ah

Being a recently established, man-made holiday, Yom ha-Sho'ah contains no prophetic significance. Even so, the events of the Holocaust do provide, in miniature, a glimpse of a yet future persecution of the people of Israel.

The Bible teaches that following the Rapture (catching up) of the church (1 Th. 4:15-17), the "prince that shall come" (or Antichrist) [Dan. 9:26] will make a seven-year covenant with the nation of Israel (Dan. 9:27). In the middle of that seven-year period the Antichrist will implement a satanically inspired (Rev. 12:13) plan of destruction against the Jewish people and the nation of Israel such as the world has never seen (Dan. 12:1). It is referred to in the Scriptures as "the time of Jacob's trouble" (Jer. 30:7) or the "great tribulation" (Mt. 24:21). By the end of this calamitous period, two-thirds of the Jewish people will have lost their lives (Zech. 13:8). The remaining one-third will be spiritually refined and become the believing remnant at the return of Jesus Christ (Zech. 13:9).

ENDNOTES

[1] Elie Wiesel, *Night* (New York: Avon Books, 1969), 44.

[2] Raul Hilberg, *The Destruction of the European Jews* (Chicago: Quadrangle Books, Inc., 1961; New York: Franklin Watts, Inc., 1973), 54.

[3] *Encyclopaedia Judaica*, 16 vols. (Jerusalem: Keter Publishing House Ltd., 1971), 8:916.

The Israeli Flag and
the Emblem of the
State of Israel

12

YOM HA-ATZMA'UT: ISRAEL'S INDEPENDENCE DAY

> So long as still within our breasts
> the Jewish heart beats true,
> So long as still towards the East,
> to Zion, looks the Jew,
> So long our hopes are not yet lost—
> two thousand years we cherished them—
> To live in freedom in the Land
> of Zion and Jerusalem.[1]

*H*atikvah, Israel's national anthem, expresses the dream that Jewish people have had for centuries—restoration to their homeland and the rebirth of their nation. On May 14, 1948, that dream became a reality. The provisional government of the modern State of Israel declared its independence, and a new nation was born. To commemorate that momentous event, a national holiday was established. It is the Israeli *4th of July* and is known as *Yom ha-Atzma'ut* (lit., *Day of the Independence*).

Origin and Description of Yom ha-Atzma'ut

To understand the significance of Yom ha-Atzma'ut to Jewish people, we must go back to an important transaction that took place between God and Abraham. "And the LORD said unto Abram, after Lot was separated from him, Lift up now thine eyes, and look from the place where thou art northward, and southward, and eastward, and westward, For all the land which thou seest, to thee will I give it, and to thy seed forever…Arise, walk through the land in the length of it and in the breadth of it; for I will give it unto thee" (Gen. 13:14-15, 17).

Amplified in other portions of Scripture, the implications of this promise are clear. Regardless of how often the Jewish people are disobedient to God, the land of Israel is still theirs. God has given it to them. Although they may not always possess the land or dwell in it, the title deed to that property still belongs to them. Although the owners may be absent for a time, God will always bring them back home. A brief look at Israel's history validates this point.

In biblical days, the people of ancient Israel were taken into captivity by the Assyrians and the Babylonians because of their rebellion against God. But God in His faithfulness brought a remnant back to the land. Later, as a direct consequence of rejecting their Messiah, Israel was once again thrust from the land of their forefathers and scattered throughout the world. The land itself was occupied by foreign peoples for nearly two thousand years.

During the final two decades of the 19th century, Israel's long dispersion started to come to an end. Small numbers of Jewish people had always lived in the land, but it was at that time that immigration to the land began to swell, primarily due to increased persecution in czarist Russia. Theodor Herzl, an Austrian newspaper reporter, led the movement to establish a Jewish homeland. Through his vision ("If you will it, it is no dream"), the world's Jewish community was mobilized to implement the *Zionist* goal—the establishment of a Jewish homeland in the ancient land of Zion, or Israel.

After World War I, the British government, then in control of Palestine, attempted to stifle further Jewish immigration, although they had earlier committed themselves to helping create a Jewish homeland. By 1947 the British were tired of placating the Arabs and penalizing the Jews in Palestine, so they turned over the responsibility of Palestine to the United Nations.

In November of that year the United Nations voted to partition Palestine into two separate states—one Arab and one Jewish. The Jewish population greeted the partition vote with dancing in the streets. The Arab community, on the other hand, rejected the plan. As the British pulled out of Palestine in May 1948, a new era dawned for Jewish people everywhere. A sense of national pride swept world Jewry as the revived State of Israel declared its independence on May 14. God's ancient people were home again.

The holiday of Yom ha-Atzma'ut was officially declared in 1949. The 5th of Iyyar (April-May), the day the Declaration of Independence was proclaimed, became the national date of the observance.

Observance of Yom ha-Atzma'ut

In Israel, the celebration of Yom ha-Atzma'ut is preceded by the solemnity of *Yom ha-Zikkaron* (lit., *Day of the Remembrance*). Held on the previous day, Iyyar 4, Yom ha-Zikkaron is a memorial day in remembrance of Israeli soldiers who fell in the line of duty.

At sunset, as Yom ha-Zikkaron draws to an end and Yom ha-Atzma'ut begins, the mood throughout Israel dramatically changes from solemnity to joviality. Throngs of people jam the streets walking, singing, and dancing. Official ceremonies are held at Mount Herzl, where the "father of Zionism" is buried. These include a gun salute marking each year of independence since 1948, as well as the lighting of 12 torches representing the 12 tribes of Israel. As with the celebration of America's Independence Day, fireworks play a big role in the Israeli celebration of Yom ha-Atzma'ut. The following day the festivities continue. There are parades highlighting Israel's young people and the land's fruitfulness, as well as family picnics and barbecues.

In the Diaspora, marking Israel's Independence Day varies from community to community. Celebrations are usually sponsored by Jewish schools, synagogues, or community centers. These festivities often include children's parades, Israeli folk dances, plays, poetry readings, the partaking of Israeli food, the retelling of the story of Israel's formation, and the recitation of the Israeli Declaration of Independence.

The patriotic overtones in the State of Israel evident during the month of Iyyar come to their fruition on the 28th day, when the holiday *Yom Yerushalayim* (lit., *Jerusalem Day*) is observed. This special day commemorates the taking of East Jerusalem by Israel during the 1967 Six-Day War. Official ceremonies include the lighting of 18 torches at the Western Wall in remembrance of the soldiers who died regaining it.

Prophecy and Yom ha-Atzma'ut

Being of such recent origin, obviously the holiday of Yom ha-Atzma'ut is not biblical and therefore has no direct prophetic implications. However, the events surrounding the holiday and the formation of the modern State of Israel do hold a significant place in the prophetic Scriptures. There are many passages in the Bible that speak of Israel's return to their homeland. Isaiah 11:11 clearly states that these restoration passages do not refer to the return of the exiles following the Babylonian captivity. Instead, Isaiah speaks of a second restoration following a second dispersion.

This truth has forced the question of whether the reemergence of the modern State of Israel should be considered a fulfillment of biblical prophecy or just the after effects of human political efforts. Ezekiel 37 helps to answer this question. In this passage, God permitted the Prophet Ezekiel to gaze into the future and behold the destiny of the Jewish nation—a destiny portrayed by a valley full of dry bones.

A careful examination of this prophecy reveals three facts.

First, the dry bones represent "the whole house of Israel" (v. 11). Second, Ezekiel states that during this episode he prophesied twice—once to the bones (v. 7) and once to the wind (v. 10). The result was also twofold. In response to the first prophecy, the bones came together, along with sinews, flesh, and skin. But there was no breath or life in them (vv. 7-8). In response to the second prophecy, breath came into the bodies giving them life (v. 10). Third, the interpretation of the vision as given by God indicates a two-phase fulfillment. The first phase sees the Lord bringing the Jewish people out of their graves and into the land of Israel (v. 12). The second phase involves a second placement of the Jews into their land, accompanied by their spiritual regeneration (v. 14).

The Scriptures therefore seem to indicate that before God fully regathers Israel from among the nations and brings them back to life spiritually, an incomplete return to the land of promise must occur, albeit in a condition of national, spiritual deadness.[2] Today's modern State of Israel is that nation regathered in unbelief. Similar to the bones of Joseph (Gen. 50:25; Ex. 13:19; Josh. 24:32), the dry bones of Ezekiel's vision have been returned to their homeland.

Prophetically speaking, the holiday of Yom ha-Atzma'ut commemorates the partial restoration of Israel back to the land of promise. Someday Israel will be able to celebrate the complete regathering of all its people and their new life in the Messiah.

ENDNOTES

[1] *Hatikvah*, by Naphtali Herz Imber, c. 1878.

[2] This interpretation does not injure the belief in the imminent return of Jesus Christ for the church, known as the Rapture. The partial return of Israel to her homeland in a state of unbelief did not have to occur prior to the Rapture. It could have occurred right after the Rapture and before the signing of the covenant with Israel by the Antichrist, which will begin the seven-year Tribulation period (Dan. 9:27). In God's timetable, however, Israel's return in unbelief did take place before the coming of the Lord Jesus for His bride.

Observing the Fifteenth
of Av and the
Fifteenth of Shevat

13

THE FIFTEENTH OF AV
AND
THE FIFTEENTH OF SHEVAT

I think that I shall never see
　　A poem lovely as a tree.
A tree whose hungry mouth is prest
　　Against the earth's sweet flowing breast;
A tree that looks at God all day,
　　And lifts her leafy arms to pray;
A tree that may in Summer wear
　　A nest of robins in her hair;
Upon whose bosom snow has lain;
　　Who intimately lives with rain.
Poems are made by fools like me,
　　But only God can make a tree.[1]

This lovely poem by Joyce Kilmer captures the essence of one of God's most beautiful creations—the tree.　Two of Israel's ancient holidays focus on trees—the place of trees in the service of God and in the reclamation of that which was spoiled.　The festivals are known as the Fifteenth of Av and the Fifteenth of Shevat.

The Fifteenth of Av

The fifteenth day of the Jewish month of Av (July–August) is a holiday instituted by the ancient rabbis, not by God, and is not found in Scripture. It is a minor holiday and observed more during the time of the Second Temple than it is today. It is a happy occasion commemorating a number of events in Jewish history.

First, the Fifteenth of Av commemorated the end of the wood-chopping season and the bringing of the last wood offering to the Temple. This wood offering was used to keep the fires of the bronze altar burning continuously, as outlined in Leviticus 6:12–13. In his day, Nehemiah reorganized and reinstituted this bringing of the wood offering (Neh. 10:34). Certain families were assigned to furnish the wood offering on this date, but everyone was welcome to voluntarily bring wood. It was a joyful time with singing, laughter, and the lighting of torches and bonfires.

The Fifteenth of Av was also called the Day of the Breaking of the Ax. No more trees were cut down for use in the Temple service after that date because the chopped wood for the altar would not have sufficient time to dry in the waning months of summer. With the destruction of the Temple and the bronze altar, the bringing of the wood offering ended in A.D. 70.

A second happy event is commemorated on the Fifteenth of Av. In Temple days a joyous incident took place on this date and was repeated on the Day of Atonement. All of the young maidens from Jerusalem dressed in white garments and sang and danced in the vineyards. This was a matrimonial dance. All of the young bachelors would look at the dancing maidens and select their brides.

A third event celebrated on the Fifteenth of Av took place in A.D. 135. The Jewish false messiah, Bar Kochba, was defeated in his insurrection by the Romans at the city of Betar. The defeat took place around the ninth of Av; however, Roman orders forbade the interment of the scores of Jews slain in battle. These orders were later rescinded, allowing for the proper burial of Israel's fallen soldiers. The date of this reversal of orders is said to have been the Fifteenth of Av.

Although in Temple times the Fifteenth of Av was a full festival, today there are few customs associated with the holiday, and these are observed by only the most zealous in the Jewish community. No eulogies or penitential prayers are said. Rather, people are encouraged to spend the day studying the Bible and rabbinical teachings.

The Fifteenth of Shevat

Like the Fifteenth of Av, the fifteenth day of the Jewish month Shevat (January–February) is also a holiday instituted by the ancient rabbis. Another minor festival, it also did not originate with God nor is any mention of it found in Scripture.

Initially, the Fifteenth of Shevat (more commonly called by its Hebrew name, *T'u B'Shevat*) was one of the four Jewish New Year's Days (see chapter on Rosh Hashanah). For the purpose of tithing fruit (cp. Neh. 10:35), it marked the beginning of the festival of the New Year of Trees (fruit trees, to be exact). Because there is no longer a Temple to which people may bring a tithe of fruit, the Fifteenth of Shevat has taken on a new meaning. It has become Israel's Arbor Day.

When the Romans defeated the Jews in the historic wars of A.D. 70 and A.D. 135, the Romans devastated the countryside by cutting down scores of trees. They stripped the landscape, not only to terrorize the Jews, but to make the land uninhabitable. The effect lasted for centuries. Even Mark Twain, when traveling through the Holy Land in 1867, commented on the barrenness of the terrain:

Of all the lands there are for dismal scenery, I
think Palestine must be the prince. The hills are
barren, they are dull of color, they are unpic-
turesque in shape. The valleys are unsightly
deserts fringed with a feeble vegetation that has an
expression about it of being sorrowful and
despondent....Every outline is harsh, every feature is distinct, there is no perspective—distance
works no enchantment here. It is a hopeless, dreary, heartbroken land.[2]

If Mark Twain could see the country of Israel today, he probably would have a different opinion. That "hopeless, dreary, heartbroken land" has been reclaimed. Before, the land was nothing
but swamps, rocks, and sand. Now the desert blossoms with
more than three thousand species of plants and flowers, including
an abundance of evergreen and fruit trees. Citrus fruits have
become Israel's second largest export. Land reclamation organi-
zations, such as the Jewish National Fund, have planted millions
of trees to reforest the country's hillsides. Israel today is a beautiful, green garden.

On Israel's Arbor Day, the Fifteenth of Shevat, the children
have the day off from school and spend their time planting trees
and singing songs. The shared experience is used to help create
fidelity to the homeland. Adults also get involved in the tree planting, and those who cannot participate give financially toward the
reforestation efforts. Outside of Israel the Fifteenth of Shevat is
observed in a variety of ways. Some people have developed their
own seder for this occasion, similar to the Passover seder. Others
follow the custom of eating 15 different kinds of fruit, particularly those fruits native to the land of Israel, such as carob.

Prophetically, the Fifteenth of Shevat plays no role in
Scripture. Still the Bible does refer to the days of the Messiah's

reign on earth when God promised:

> *I will multiply the fruit of the tree...the desolate land shall be tilled, whereas it lay desolate in the sight of all that passed by. And they shall say, This land that was desolate is become like the garden of Eden, and the waste and desolate and ruined cities are become fortified, and are inhabited. Then the nations that are left round about you shall know that I, the LORD, build the ruined places, and plant that which was desolate. I, the LORD, have spoken it, and I will do it* (Ezek. 36:30, 34–36).

ENDNOTES

[1] Hazel Felleman, comp., *The Best Loved Poems of the American People* (New York: Doubleday, 1936), 561.

[2] Mark Twain, *The Innocents Abroad*, 2 vols. (New York: Harper & Row, Publishers, 1869), 2:357.

Prayer ane Fasting during The Fast Days of Israel

14

THE FAST DAYS
OF ISRAEL

The ancient rabbis taught that each generation of Jews has the capacity to bring about the final redemption of Israel. In Jewish tradition, fasting (abstaining from food for ritual purposes) is seen as the means to repentance, which, subsequently, is the means to the final redemption. Thus, great importance is placed on the establishment and observance of Israel's fast days.

Biblical Fasting

There are 56 references to voluntary fasting in the Bible. Apart from the prophetic references in Joel 1:14; 2:12; and 2:15, there is no direct command found anywhere in Scripture that people should fast. Even so, there are numerous instances where fasting was practiced, even by the Lord Jesus (Mt. 4:2). The Word of God reveals the primary purpose of fasting: "And he [God] humbled thee, and suffered thee to hunger, and fed thee with manna, which thou knewest not, neither did thy fathers know; that he might make thee know that man doth not live by bread only, but by every word that proceedeth out of the mouth of the LORD doth man live" (Dt. 8:3).

Fasting does nothing for God. It does not impress Him, nor does it enable people to earn merit with Him. Fasting is for mankind's benefit, that people may learn an attitude of dependence on God, not just for daily bread but, more importantly, for proper living according to His Word. This is clearly spelled out in Isaiah 58:1–12, where the Lord uncovers the hypocrisy often associated with fasting and other outward religious rituals. God is not pleased with the kind of fasting by which people demean and afflict themselves to the point of degradation (v. 5). Church history is strewn with accounts of people who sought personal holiness and favor with God by living in caves, sitting atop poles, and grazing like cattle. Rather, the Lord desires the kind of fasting evidenced by godly behavior. "Is not this the fast that I have chosen—to loose the bands of wickedness, to undo the heavy burdens, and to let the oppressed go free, and that ye break every yoke?" (Isa. 58:6).

The lesson from the Word of God is apparent: True humility expresses itself, not in self-abasement, but in serving others. Our best example of such humility is Jesus Christ (Phil. 2:5–8).

Jewish Fasts

Fasting within rabbinical Judaism goes back to biblical days. The self-righteous Pharisee of Luke 18 was proud of the fact that he fasted twice a week. This was not done out of obedience to a biblical injunction but rather out of deference to a man-made custom. In Jewish tradition, Moses ascended into heaven to receive the law on a Thursday and descended on a Monday. It therefore became common to fast on those days. Orthodox Jews still keep this tradition.

There are both private and public Jewish fasts. The Reform branch of Judaism, however, does not acknowledge any fast other than the one on the Day of Atonement.

Fast of the Firstborn

Possibly originating as early as A.D. 200, the Fast of the Firstborn is a private fast. It is observed by the firstborn male in each household in commemoration and gratitude for the firstborn males who were spared by God on the first Passover night in Egypt. The fast takes place on Nisan 14 (March–April), the day before the Feast of Unleavened Bread begins.

Fast of Esther

The Fast of Esther is a public fast observed on Adar 13 (February–March). It is held in memory of the fast the Jews in Susa engaged in, at the request of Queen Esther, before she sought entrance to King Ahasuerus (Est. 4:16).

There are four Jewish fasts commemorating the destruction of the First and Second Temples: The Fast of the Tenth of Tevet, the Fast of the Seventeenth of Tammuz, the Fast of Gedaliah, and the Fast of Tisha B'Av (Ninth of Av). Although they are referred to in Scripture (Zech 8:19), all four are man-made fasts implemented after 586 B.C., when the Babylonians destroyed Solomon's Temple.

We will look at the first three fasts briefly, while the fourth, the Fast of the Ninth of Av, will be examined in detail.

Fast of the Tenth of Tevet

The Fast of the Tenth of Tevet (December–January) memorializes the onset of the siege of Jerusalem by King Nebuchadnezzar (2 Ki. 25:1). It marks the beginning of the end of Israel's first commonwealth and First Temple. It is the fast referred to in Zechariah 8:19 as "the fast of the tenth [month]."

Fast of the Seventeenth of Tammuz

Alluded to as "the fast of the fourth month" in Zechariah 8:19, the Fast of the Seventeenth of Tammuz (June–July) was originally instituted to remember the day the walls of Jerusalem were broken by the Babylonian army (Jer. 52:6–7). Since the walls were actually breached on the ninth of the month, it is likely that the fast was initially observed on that date. Later, after the destruction of Jerusalem and the Temple by the Roman army, the date was changed to the 17th. The reason is twofold. First, the daily Temple sacrifice was halted during the Roman siege on the 17th of Tammuz; and second, because the Second Temple destruction is seen in Jewish tradition as the greater disaster, the two commemorative dates were combined into one, with the 17th taking precedence.

Fast of Gedaliah

After King Nebuchadnezzar defeated the Judeans and took them into captivity, he appointed a Jewish man named Gedaliah to be governor of the small populace left behind. Unfortunately, in the seventh month, Tishri (September–October), Gedaliah was assassinated (Jer. 41). After his death, a fast was invoked to memorialize him and the end of the first Jewish commonwealth. This Fast of Gedaliah is "the fast of the seventh month" mentioned in Zechariah 7:5 and 8:19 and is observed on the third of Tishri.

Fast of Tisha B'Av (Ninth of Av)

"He who does not mourn over the Destruction of Zion will not live to see her joy."[1] Passed down through the ages, this rabbinical saying encapsulates the essence of one of the gloomiest days on the Jewish calendar—Tisha B'Av. Tisha B'Av, or the Ninth of Av (July-August), not only commemorates specific tragedies in Jewish history, it also symbolizes all that has been dismal, dreadful, and lamentable in Jewish existence. It is the Jewish *Friday the 13th*.

Origin and Description of Tisha B'Av

By comparing Zechariah 8:19 and 7:3, 5, there is indication that Tisha B'Av was instituted some time after the fall of

Jerusalem in 586 B.C. At the same time, the Bible gives no evidence that Tisha B'Av, as a commemorative fast day, had its source with God or received any form of divine sanction.

Tisha B'Av marks the destruction of both the First and Second Temples in Jerusalem. The First Temple was destroyed in 586 B.C. by the Babylonians. The Second Temple was destroyed by the Romans in A.D. 70. Neither calamity occurred on the Ninth of Av. Jewish tradition determined, however, that both events would be remembered on that date to coincide with other Jewish disasters that fell either on or near the same date.

For instance, in A.D. 132 the Jewish community in Israel revolted against Rome for the second time. Under the leadership of a false messiah named Bar Kochba, the Jewish army held out for three years. Their last stronghold, the city of Betar, fell in A.D. 135 on the Ninth of Av. Exactly one year later, again on the Ninth of Av, the Roman emperor Hadrian had the ruins of the city of Jerusalem plowed under by a team of oxen. He then built a Roman city on the site and called it Aelia Capitolina. All Jews were forbidden to enter the city upon penalty of death. Other calamities associated with Tisha B'Av include the burning of Talmud books at Paris in 1242; the expulsion of thousands of Jews from Spain in 1492, thus ending Spanish Jewry's "Golden Age"; and the deportation of Jews from the Warsaw Ghetto to the Treblinka death camp in 1942.

It is "For these things I weep" (Lam. 1:16), says the Jewish soul on Tisha B'Av.

Observance of Tisha B'Av

There are few recorded details about the observance of Tisha B'Av in biblical days. Zechariah states that people wept and mourned on the Ninth of Av (7:3–5). The returned Jewish exiles also "separated" themselves on that date (7:3). The idea was to abstain or set themselves apart from certain things for the purpose of consecration. Fasting was thought to be one way to accomplish this.

Today Tisha B'Av is observed by fasting, abstaining from work, and sitting and sleeping on the ground (cp. Lam. 2:10). Except for certain "mournful" portions, studying the Scriptures is also prohibited because "The statutes of the Lord are right, rejoicing the heart" (Ps. 19:8). Because rejoicing is forbidden on Tisha B'Av, studying God's Word on that day would violate that prohibition.

The solemnity of Tisha B'Av is carried over into the synagogue. During the evening service the synagogue is lit by the light of only one lamp (cp. Lam. 3:6). The Book of Lamentations is read, along with various prayers.

The Sabbath immediately following Tisha B'Av is called the "Comfort Sabbath" because the Prophets' portion of the reading for that day, Isaiah 40:1-26, begins with the word "Comfort." It seems fitting that the sorrowing Jewish mind, after recalling the painful past of Tisha B'Av, should be consoled with the words, "Comfort ye, comfort ye my people, saith your God."

Prophecy and Tisha B'Av

Being a man-made holiday, Tisha B'Av does not figure into biblical prophecy in a significant way. There are certain predictions, however, that relate to Tisha B'Av's background and future.

The original intent of the Fast of Tisha B'Av was to remember the destruction of the First Temple. Years later, the memorial was also applied to the laying waste of the Second Temple. Both catastrophes were foreseen in Scripture (1 Ki. 9:7; Mt. 24:1–2). Along with the prophecies, the reasons for the Temple calamities were also made plain in Scripture. "For the sins of Manasseh" (2 Ki. 24:3) God removed Judah "out of his sight" and had the First Temple destroyed. These sins included idolatry, child sacrifice, occult practices, and shedding innocent blood (2 Ki. 21:3, 6, 16). The devastation of the Second Temple was due to Israel's inability to know "the time of [its] visitation [by the Messiah]" (Lk. 19:44). The result was its subsequent rejection of Him. The Bible is clear. Both Temple destructions were not only foreseen but openly declared. Ample warning was given. When applied to the Bible, the saying is true, "Coming events cast their shadows before."

The Word of God gives a much brighter picture of what will become of Tisha B'Av in the future. "Thus saith the LORD of hosts: The fast of the fourth month, and the fast of the fifth, and the fast of the seventh, and the fast of the tenth, shall be to the house of Judah joy and gladness, and cheerful feasts" (Zech. 8:19).

In the days of the Messiah, instead of being a fast, God will transform Tisha B'Av (along with the Fast of the Seventeenth of Tammuz, the Fast of Gedaliah, and the Fast of the Tenth of Tevet) into a feast—a cheerful feast! Instead of weeping, there will be joy. Instead of mourning, there will be gladness. The entire purpose and practice of Israel's saddest day of the year will be completely refurbished. No longer will people and nations recall the old Jerusalem with its tortured past. In the future there will be a new, rejuvenated Jerusalem. "There shall yet old men and old women dwell in the streets of [that] Jerusalem, and every man with his staff in his hand for very age. And the streets of the city shall be full of boys and girls playing in the streets of it" (Zech. 8:4-5).

Until that time, the Word of God offers Israel a benevolent exhortation. Although Tisha B'Av now brings sorrow to the heart and tears to the eyes, one day it will bring joy and laughter. The Lord has promised "to do good unto Jerusalem and to the house of Judah; fear ye not" (Zech. 8:15).

ENDNOTE

[1] Nathan Ausubel, *The Book of Jewish Knowledge* (New York: Crown Publishers, Inc., 1964), 469.

Shadow or Substance?

15

SHADOW OR SUBSTANCE?

In a study of the Jewish festivals people may ask, Should Christians observe these holidays? Or, should Christians observe any religious festivals at all? The Bible gives the answers to these and other related questions.

As Christians, must we observe religious festivals?

There is no evidence in the New Testament that Christians are obligated to keep any religious festival. Apart from two ordinances established by the Lord Jesus (baptism and the Lord's Supper or Communion), there is no commandment in Scripture requiring the body of Christ to observe any of the biblical festivals, and certainly there is no obligation to observe any of the nonbiblical or man-made festivals.

Christians presently are not under the law of Moses but under grace (Rom. 6:14) and therefore are not expected to keep any form of ritual or holiday observance. Furthermore, just because there will be festival observances during the millennial reign of the Messiah, it does not follow that we are to do the same during the church age. There are exceptions found in the New Testament, instances where Christians kept Old Testament laws (Acts 21:20) or met consistently on a certain day for worship (Acts 20:7). These were merely customs, not commandments. Customs are commonly accepted forms of behavior; they are not obligatory in God's eyes.

The Apostle Peter, who once took great pride in keeping himself ritually pure (Acts 10:14), asked a pointed question of those believers who emphasized the law of Moses. During the great Jerusalem Council of Acts 15, Peter inquired, "Now, therefore, why put God to the test, to put a yoke upon the neck of the disciples, which neither our fathers nor we were able to bear?" (Acts 15:10). Requiring Christians to keep any type of religious festival is not only putting on them an unbearable yoke, it is also testing God.

The Apostle Paul spent a good part of his ministry combating the idea that believers in Jesus Christ are obligated to keep religious codes and laws. If we allow ourselves to fall into that trap, Paul's words to the Galatians could very well be applied to us as well: "O foolish Galatians, who hath bewitched you . . .?" (Gal. 3:1).

As Christians, may we observe religious festivals?

Although we are not obligated to keep religious festivals, we may do so if we wish. Being free in Christ means just that. We have the choice of celebrating certain holidays, be they Passover, Easter, Hanukkah, Christmas, or whatever. Many Christians celebrate religious holidays if for no other reason than to forge family memories and create unity and cohesion in the home. Family gatherings focusing on a central theme or activity, such as a holiday, often help to accomplish this unity.

The freedom we have in Christ allows us to keep any of a number of different holidays. God does not require us to observe any holiday, but if it is our desire to do so, He gives us that latitude, within biblical parameters. The Apostle Paul set forth a guiding principle in making such a decision: "All things are lawful unto me, but all things are not expedient; all things are lawful for me, but I will not be brought under the power of any...all things are lawful for me, but all things edify not" (1 Cor. 6:12; 10:23b).

This brings us to our final question.

As Christians, should we observe religious festivals?

First, we should not observe any religious festival that demotes or denies Scripture.

In Matthew 15 and Mark 7, Jesus rebuked the religious leaders of His day because they relegated the Word of God to a position beneath that of the tradition of men. Jesus declared, "For laying aside the commandment of God, ye hold the tradition of men...Full well ye reject the commandment of God, that ye may keep your own tradition...Making the word of God of no effect through your tradition" (Mk. 7:8, 9, 13).

The same mistake can be seen today in the observance of the Sabbath. One Jewish author writes concerning carrying an object on the Sabbath:

> We have already noted the deplorable ignorance and neglect among large sections of the Jewish public of these laws against carrying on Sabbath. Yet, as we have seen, they are of fundamental importance in the Sabbath scheme. Our Sages have decreed that the [commandments] of [carrying the] shofar and lulav [during the Feast of Tabernacles] shall not be observed if the occasion for performing them falls on Sabbath. The only reason for this decree is: lest an over-enthusiastic Jew might forget it was Sabbath and inadvertently carry the shofar or the lulav in the street. Our great teachers considered the mere possibility of a desecration of the Sabbath by carrying to be of such consequence that they decreed the

> omission of these two important [commandments]
> of the Torah rather than take that risk.[1]

In this example, the ancient rabbis have nullified the Word of God regarding the Feast of Tabernacles for the sake of their own tradition. Christians should not observe a religious festival if it requires them to demote the Word of God in this way.

Christians also should be careful of engaging in a religious festival if it requires them to deny the Word of God. For example, one of the benedictions recited at the opening of many of the Jewish holidays is, "Blessed art thou, O Lord our God, King of the universe, who hast hallowed us by Thy commandments, and hast commanded us to kindle the Festival light."[2] God has not commanded us to kindle the festival light. There is no Scripture that requires the lighting of candles on any of the biblical holidays. It is a man-made custom that has been falsely accredited with divine sanction. This goes directly against Proverbs 30:5–6: "Every word of God is pure…Add thou not unto his words, lest he reprove thee, and thou be found a liar."

We as Christians should not keep a festival or a custom within a festival if it demotes or denies the Word of God.

A second reason for not observing a religious festival is if we expect any spiritual benefit from it, other than pointing us to Christ.

For example, some Christians keep religious festivals as a means of preserving their rich cultural heritage. They may be unaware that in so doing they are elevating their ethnic and cultural background above that of their identity in Christ.

The Bible states that once people accept Jesus the Messiah as their personal Savior, they then receive a new identity. Whatever their previous background—Jewish, Gentile, slave, free, male, female (Gal. 3:28)—when people put their trust in Christ, none of that matters anymore. The only thing that matters is that they are now "in Christ."

Being "in Christ" does not mean that people of Jewish, Swedish, German, or any other ethnic background somehow lose their historical legacy—just as it does not mean that a man stops being a man or a woman stops being a woman. Being "in Christ" means that individuals define themselves, people identify themselves, not based on their past, their family tree, their status in life, or their religious heritage. Rather, their identity is based solely on their biblically prescribed position in Jesus Christ.

Two of the greatest men of the Bible realized that who they were did not depend on exterior standards. Moses, who had been given the Torah with all of its rituals and laws, did not define his own identity nor that of Israel by these outward things, but rather by the presence of God in his life. In Exodus 33:16 Moses said to the Lord, "For wherein shall it be known here that I and thy people have found grace in thy sight? Is it not in that thou goest with us? So shall we be separated, I and thy people, from all the people that are upon the face of the earth."

In the New Testament the Apostle Paul outlined his great religious pedigree: "Circumcised the eighth day, of the stock of Israel, of the tribe of Benjamin, an Hebrew of the Hebrews; as touching the law, a Pharisee; Concerning zeal, persecuting the church; touching the righteousness which is in the law, blameless" (Phil. 3:5–6).

But as a new creature in Christ, none of these things mattered to Paul. "But what things were gain to me, those I counted loss for Christ. Yea doubtless, and I count all things but loss for the excellency of the knowledge of Christ Jesus, my Lord; for whom I have suffered the loss of all things, and do count them but refuse, that I may win Christ, And be found in him" (Phil. 3:7–9a).

We learn from the Word of God, then, that if Christians are keeping religious festivals just to hold on to some facet of their cultural identity, they are missing out on God's best. Culture is not a substitute for Christ.

Another benefit some Christians expect from observing

religious festivals is spiritual growth. They think that keeping certain rituals and customs will help them mature in their faith. They are mistaken (see Gal. 2:21; Phil. 3:9).

On numerous occasions the Apostle Paul reprimanded his brothers and sisters in Christ for thinking that outward rituals had anything to do with their sanctification—their progressive transformation into the image and likeness of Jesus Christ. Paul stated that those who rely on religious ceremonies are "weak in the faith" (Rom. 14:1). He worried that his ministry may have been in vain because his readers were caught up in the observance of special occasions. "But now, after ye have known God, or rather are known by God, how turn ye again to the weak and beggarly elements, unto which ye desire again to be in bondage? Ye observe days, and months, and times, and years. I am afraid of you, lest I have bestowed upon you labor in vain" (Gal. 4:9–11).

Paul wondered why Christians would submit themselves to religious regulations that offer no help of spiritual victory. "Wherefore, if ye be dead with Christ from the rudiments of the world, why, as though living in the world, are ye subject to ordinances (Touch not; taste not; handle not; Which all are to perish with the using) after the commandments and doctrines of men? These things have indeed a show of wisdom in will-worship, and humility, and neglecting of the body, not in any honor to the satisfying of the flesh" (Col. 2:20–23).

The question remains, then, If religious festivals are spiritually weak, if they contribute nothing to spiritual maturity, if they provide no power over fleshly indulgence, why would Christians feel it necessary to observe them? What spiritual benefit would they hope to obtain?

As with the rest of the law, religious festivals may serve as object lessons to point us to Christ (Gal. 3:24), but spiritually they do little else.

A third reason for not observing religious festivals is if there are too many of them.

Numerous traditions and rituals can virtually insulate a person from that which is most important—the person of Jesus Christ. Those who do not know Jesus Christ as their Savior are often surrounded by a voluminous number of religious rules, laws, and ceremonies that effectively shield them from Jesus' claims. They do not realize that through the comfort and protection of tradition, whether or not He really is the Messiah has already been determined for them.

Christians can occupy their time with too much ceremonial patronage. The observance of various festivals, along with other religious obligations, may keep us spiritually active, but the cost is often abandonment of our "first love" (Rev. 2:4).

A fourth reason for not observing a religious festival is if it cannot be celebrated with sincerity.

The danger with oft-repeated rituals is that they can lose their meaning. They turn into purposeless habits performed by rote. This was the condition of ancient Israel. Their mindless repetition when observing the festivals, coupled with their hypocritical lifestyles, disgusted God. "Bring no more vain oblations; incense is an abomination unto me; the new moons and sabbaths, the calling of assemblies, I cannot bear; it is iniquity, even the solemn meeting. Your new moons and your appointed feasts my soul hateth; they are a trouble unto me; I am weary of bearing them" (Isa. 1:13–14; cp. Amos 5:21). Because of their disobedience and insincerity, Israel eventually lost the privilege of observing their holidays altogether (Hos. 2:11; Lam. 2:6).

Christians also can make the same mistake. Like ancient Israel, our hearts can be far from the Lord, even as we move our lips in perfect time to the accepted code of conduct (Isa. 29:13). If we are not careful, proper observance and form can become our primary concerns, leading to legalism. God is not concerned that we are dutiful in superficial liturgies; rather, He wants us to know and worship Him "in spirit and in truth" (Jn. 4:24). Our God calls us to something far better than the observance of mere religious festivals. He calls us to spiritual authenticity that comes from the heart and finds its fountainhead in Him.

Despite these potential hazards in observing religious festivals, the reality is that many Christians still participate in them. We therefore must avoid a judgmental attitude among the brethren. Those who commemorate a holiday must not judge those who do not, and those who do not commemorate a holiday must not judge those who do. Is this not the Apostle Paul's point in Romans? "Let not him that eateth despise him that eateth not; and let not him who eateth not judge him that eateth; for God hath received him. Who art thou that judgest another man's servant? . . . One man esteemeth one day above another; another esteemeth every day alike . . . He that regardeth the day, regardeth it unto the Lord; and he that regardeth not the day, to the Lord he doth not regard it . . . But why dost thou judge thy brother? Or why dost thou set at nought thy brother? For we shall all stand before the judgment seat of Christ" (Rom. 14:3–4a, 5, 6, 10). This point is reiterated in Colossians 2:16: "Let no man, therefore, judge you in food, or in drink, or in respect of a feast day, or of the new moon, or of a sabbath day."

When we judge our brothers and sisters in Christ for either keeping or not keeping religious festivals, we put ourselves in the place of God, to whom "every one of us shall give account of himself" (Rom. 14:12). Instead, we must relate to those with whom we disagree through love (Rom. 14:15). We must strive to "Give no offense, neither to the Jews, nor to the Greeks, nor to the church of God" (1 Cor. 10:32).

This does not mean that we should compromise our personal convictions. We must understand the issues involved. "Let every man be fully persuaded in his own mind" (Rom. 14:5). However, regarding how to treat others, our *modus operandi* is to love them and let God do the judging. At the same time, those who are "weak in the faith" (Rom. 14:1) or weak in conscience (1 Cor. 8:7) are encouraged to become strong in the faith, no longer children in their understanding (1 Cor. 14:20). As Christians, we are admonished to "henceforth be no more children, tossed to and fro, and carried about with every wind of doctrine, by the sleight of men, and cunning craftiness, by which they lie in wait to deceive; But, speaking the truth in love, may [we] grow up into him in all things, who is the head, even Christ" (Eph. 4:14-15).

When it comes to observing religious festivals, "We, then, that are strong ought to bear the infirmities of the weak, and not to please ourselves" (Rom. 15:1). And those who are weak should come to the understanding that all of the festivals, all of the new moons, and all of the Sabbath days are merely "a shadow of things to come; but the body [or substance] is of Christ" (Col. 2:17).

ENDNOTES

[1] Isidor Grunfeld, *The Sabbath* (1954; reprint, New York: Feldheim Publishers, 1988), 62.

[2] Joseph H. Hertz, *The Authorised Daily Prayer Book*, rev. ed. (New York: Bloch Publishing Co., 1948), 797.

GLOSSARY

The following guide is used for those words needing pronunciation explanation.

AH = *a* as in father

AY = *a* as in made

EE = *e* as in seen

EH = *e* as in get

I = *i* as in fit

OH = *o* as in go

OO = *oo* as in too

CH = *ch* as in Scottish *loch*

ABIB (AH-BEEB): The original name of the first month of the Jewish calendar.

ADAR (AH-DAHR): The 12th month on the Jewish religious calendar.

AFIKOMEN (AH-FEE-KOH-MAHN): The broken piece of matzo hidden and found during the Passover seder.

ATZERET (AH-TZEH-REHT): A solemn assembly, sometimes referring to the Feast of Pentecost.

AV (AHV): The fifth month of the Jewish religious calendar.

AVODAH (AH-VOH-DAH): The liturgy followed on Yom Kippur, recounting the duties of the high priest on the Day of Atonement.

AZAZEL (AH-ZAH-ZEHL): The scapegoat on the Day of Atonement.

BAR KOCHBA (BAHR KOHCH-BAH): A Jewish false messiah defeated by the Romans in A.D. 135.

BEMA (BEE-MAH): The platform in the synagogue from which the Torah scroll is read.

CANTOR: The synagogue official who leads the congregation in the songs and prayers.

CHAROSET (CHAH-ROH-SEHT): A mixture of chopped apples, nuts, cinnamon, and wine or grape juice eaten during the Passover seder.

CHATAN BERESIIIT (CHAN-TAHN BEH-REH-SHEET): The title given to the reader of the first portion of the Torah during Simchat Torah.

CHATAN TORAH (CHAN-TAHN TOH-RAH): The title given to the reader of the last portion of the Torah during Simchat Torah.

CHESHVAN (CHEHSH-VAHN): The eighth month of the Jewish religious calendar.

DIASPORA: Jewish communities outside of the land of Israel.

DREIDEL (DRAY-DEHL): A four-sided top used during the festival of Hanukkah.

ELUL (EH-LOOL): The sixth month of the Jewish religious calendar.

ERUV (EH-ROOV): A portion of food prepared ahead of time and placed strategically at the Sabbath limits. It also can refer to the demarcation between a private domain and a public domain.

ETROG (EHT-ROHG): The citrus fruit carried during the Feast of Tabernacles.

GELT (GEHLT): Chocolate shaped like coins or actual coins given to children during the festival of Hanukkah.

GREGGERS (GRAHG-GERS): Noisemakers used during the festival of Purim.

GUT SHABES (GOOT SHAH-BEHS): A greeting on the Sabbath meaning *Good Sabbath*.

GUT YONTEV (GOOT YAHN-TEHV): A greeting meaning *Good Holiday.*

HADASSAH (HAH-DAHS-SAH): The Hebrew name of Queen Esther.

HAGGADAH (HAHG-GAH-DAH): A booklet used during the Passover seder containing the Exodus story, rabbinical commentaries, and assorted prayers and songs.

HAKKAFOT (HAHK-KAH-FOHT): The procession of carrying the Torah scroll during Simchat Torah.

HALLAH (CHAHL-LAH): Holiday bread used on the Sabbath and during other festivals.

HAMANTASHEN (HAH-MAHN-TAH-SHEHN): A three-cornered pastry eaten during the festival of Purim.

HALLEL (HAHL-LEHL): Psalms 113—118.

HAMETZ (CHAH-MEHTZ): Food products containing leaven.

HANUKKAH (CHAH-NOOK-KAH): The festival held in the Jewish month Kislev commemorating the rededication of the Temple.

HANUKKIYAH (CHAN-NOOK-KEE-YAH): The nine-branched menorah used during the festival of Hanukkah.

HATIKVAH (HAH-TIK-VAH): The Israeli national anthem.

HAVDALAH (HAHV-DAH-LAH): A farewell ceremony for the Sabbath held late Saturday afternoon.

HOSHANA RABBAH (HOH-SHAH-NAH RAH-BAH): The seventh day of the Feast of Tabernacles, known as the Great Hosanna.

IYYAR (EE-YAHR): The second month of the Jewish religious calendar.

KAPPAROT (KAHP-PAH-ROHT): The act of swinging a chicken

over the head on Yom Kippur as a substitute to atone for a person's sin.

KIBITZING (KI-BITZ-EENG): Joking or speaking lightly.

KIDDUSH (KID-DOOSH): A blessing over wine.

KISLEV (KIS-LEHV): The ninth month of the Jewish religious calendar.

KITTEL (KIT-TEHL): A white garment worn on special occasions.

KOL NIDREI (KAHL NID-REH): A prayer chanted on Yom Kippur annulling any upcoming vows.

KREPLACH (KREHP-LACH): Triangular dumplings filled with meat or cheese.

LAG BA-OMER (LAHG BAH-OH-MER): A semi-holiday commemorating the end of a plague in Jewish history.

LATKES (LAHT-KEHS): Crispy potato pancakes eaten during the festival of Hanukkah.

LULAV (LOO-LAHV): Collectively, the three species of leafy branches carried during the Feast of Tabernacles. Specifically, it refers only to the palm branch.

MACHZOR (MAHCH-ZOHR): The prayer book used on Rosh Hashanah and Yom Kippur.

MAOZ TZUR (MAH-OHZ TZOOR): A traditional Jewish hymn sung during the festival of Hanukkah.

MATZO (MAHTZ-ZAH): Unleavened bread, or crackers, used during the Passover seder and the Feast of Unleavened Bread.

MEGILLAH (MEHG-GIL-LAH): Generally, a scroll. Specifically, the scroll of the Book of Esther read during the festival of Purim.

MIDRASH RABBAH (MID-RAHSH RAH-BAH): A collection of rabbinical exegetical sermons.

MISHNAH (MISH-NAH): A collection of rabbinical commentaries

on the Old Testament.

NISAN (NEE-SAHN): The first month of the Jewish religious calendar.

OMER (OH-MER): The sheaf of first fruits waved during the Feast of Unleavened Bread.

ONEG SHABBAT (OH-NEHG SHAHB-BAHT): An informal gathering after the Sabbath evening service.

PESACH (PEH-SAHCH): The festival of Passover or, sometimes, Unleavened Bread.

PURIM (POO-REEM): The festival held in the Jewish month Adar commemorating the preservation of the Jewish people.

ROSH HASHANAH (ROHSH HAH-SHAH-NAH): The holiday celebrating the Jewish civil New Year.

ROSH HODESH (ROHSH CHOH-DEHSH): The new moon holiday.

SANHEDRIN: The 71-member governing body of Jewish religious leaders, ca. 63 B.C.—A.D. 425.

SEDER (SAY-DER): The Passover order of service.

SHABBAT (SHAHB-BAHT): The Sabbath.

SHALOM ALEICHEM (SHAH-LOHM AH-LEH-CHEHM): A greeting that means *Peace be unto you.*

SHAMMASH (SHAHM-MAHSH): The ninth or *servant* candle of the Hanukkah menorah used to light the other eight candles.

SHAVUOT (SHAH-VOO-OHT): The festival of Pentecost.

SHEMA (SHEH-MAH): The primary Jewish declaration of faith derived from Deuteronomy 6:4.

SHEMINI ATZERET (SHEH-MI-NEE AH-TZEH-REHT): The solemn assembly observed on the eighth day of the Feast of

Tabernacles.

SHEVAT (SHEH-VAHT): The 11th month of the Jewish religious calendar.

SHOFAR (SHOH-FAHR): A musical instrument fashioned from a ram's horn and blown on Rosh Hashanah.

SHUL (SHOOL): Yiddish term for the synagogue.

SIMCHAT TORAH (SIM-CHAHT TOH-RAH): The final day of the Feast of Tabernacles, observed as a festival itself, celebrating the completion of reading through the Torah.

SIVAN (SEE-VAHN): The third month of the Jewish religious calendar.

SUKKAH (SOOK-KAH): A temporary shelter or booth erected for the Feast of Tabernacles.

SUKKOT (SOOK-KOHT): The Feast of Tabernacles

TALLIT (TAHL-LEET): Jewish prayer shawls.

TALMUD (TAHL-MOOD): A collection of rabbinical commentaries, including the Mishnah and the Gemara (rabbinical commentaries on the Mishnah).

TAMMUZ (TAHM-MOOZ): The fourth month of the Jewish religious calendar.

TASHLICH (TAHSH-LEECH): A ritual on Rosh Hashanah where the contents of a person's pockets are cast into a body of water.

TEVET (TEH-VEHT): The tenth month of the Jewish religious calendar.

TISHA B'AV (TISH-AH BEH-AHV): The ninth of the Jewish month of Av, observed as a fast day.

TISHRI (TISH-REE): The seventh month of the Jewish religious calendar and the first month of the Jewish civil calendar.

TORAH (TOH-RAH): Specifically, the five books of Moses. More generally, the totality of Jewish religious literature.

T'U B'SHEVAT (TOO BI-SHEH-VAHT): The Hebrew name of the Fifteenth of Shevat festival.

YAD VASHEM (YAHD VAH-SHEHM): The National Holocaust Memorial Center in Israel.

YARMULKE (YAHR-MOOL-KEH):   A skullcap worn by Jewish males.

YOM HA-ATZMA'UT (YOHM HAH-AHTZ-MAH-OOT): The Israeli national Independence Day.

YOM HA-SHOAH (YOHM HAH-SHOH-AH): The Jewish day to commemorate the Holocaust.

YOM HA-ZIKKARON (YOHM HAH-ZIK-KAH-ROHN): The Israeli national Memorial Day.

YOM KIPPUR (YOHM KIP-POOR): The Day of Atonement.

YOM YERUSHALAYIM (YOHM YEH-ROO-SHAH-LAH-YIM): The Israeli holiday commemorating the taking of East Jerusalem during the 1967 Six-Day War.

SELECT BIBLIOGRAPHY

Ausubel, Nathan. *The Book of Jewish Knowledge*. New York: Crown Publishers, Inc., 1964.

The Babylonian Talmud. Translated under the editorship of I. Epstein, *et al.* 18 vols. London: The Soncino Press, 1938.

Berlin, Meyer, *et al*, eds. *Encyclopedia Talmudica*. 3 vols. Jerusalem: Talmudic Encyclopedia Institute, 1978.

Bloch, Abraham P. *The Biblical and Historical Background of the Jewish Holy Days*. New York: Ktav Publishing House, Inc., 1978.

Buksbazen, Victor. *The Gospel in the Feasts of Israel*. Bellmawr, NJ: The Friends of Israel Gospel Ministry, Inc., 1954.

Cardozo, Arlene Rossen. *Jewish Family Celebrations: The Sabbath, Festivals, and Ceremonies*. New York: St. Martin's Press, 1982.

DeHaan, Richard W. *Israel and the Nations in Prophecy*. Grand Rapids: Zondervan Publishing House, 1968.

Eckstein, Yechiel. *What Christians Should Know About Jews and Judaism*. Waco: Word Books, Inc., 1984.

Edersheim, Alfred. *The Life and Times of Jesus the Messiah*. 2 vols. 1883. Reprint (2 vols. in 1). Grand Rapids: Wm. B. Eerdmans Publishing Co., 1981.

Encyclopaedia Judaica. 16 vols. Jerusalem: Keter Publishing House, Ltd., 1971.

Finegan, Jack. *Light from the Ancient Past: The Archaeological Background of Judaism and Christianity*. 2 vols. Princeton: Princeton University Press, 1959.

Ganzfried, Solomon. *Code of Jewish Law*. Translated by Hyman E. Goldin. Rev. ed. (4 vols. In 1). New York: Hebrew Publishing

Co., 1961.

Ginzberg, Louis. *The Legends of the Jews.* 7 vols. Philadelphia: The Jewish Publication Society of America, 1909-38.

Goodman, Philip. *The Purim Anthology.* Philadelphia: The Jewish Publication Society of America, 1964.

————. *The Passover Anthology.* Philadelphia: The Jewish Publication Society of America, 1966.

Grayzel, Solomon. *A History of the Jews: From the Babylonian Exile to the Establishment of Israel.* Philadelphia: The Jewish Publication Society of America, 1955.

Grunfeld, Isidor. *The Sabbath.* 1954. Reprint. New York: Feldheim Publishers, 1988.

Hertz, Joseph H. *The Authorised Daily Prayer Book.* Rev. ed. New York: Bloch Publishing Co., 1948.

————, ed. *The Pentateuch and Haftorahs.* 2nd ed. London: The Soncino Press, 1970.

Hilberg, Raul. *The Destruction of the European Jews.* Chicago: Quadrangle Books, Inc., 1961; New York: Franklin Watts, Inc., 1973.

Israel My Glory, December/January 1989-90; April/May 1991; June/July 1991; August/September 1991; April/May 1992.

Josephus. Translated by William Whiston. Grand Rapids: Kregel Publications, 1960.

Kitov, Eliyahu. *The Book of Our Heritage.* Translated by Nathan Bulman. 3 vols. Rev. ed. Jerusalem: Feldheim Publishers, 1978.

Kolatch, Alfred J. *The Jewish Book of Why.* Middle Village, NY: Jonathan David Publishers, Inc., 1981.

Lengyel, Olga. *Five Chimneys: The Story of Auschwitz.* Chicago: Ziff-Davis Publishing Co., 1947.

Midrash Rabbah. Translated by H. Freedman. 10 vols. 3rd ed.

New York: The Soncino Press, 1983.

The Mishnah. Translated by Herbert Danby. New York: Oxford University Press, 1933.

Posner, Raphael, *et al*, eds. *Jewish Liturgy: Prayer and Synagogue Service Through the Ages.* New York: Leon Amiel Publisher, 1975.

Rosenberg, David. *Chosen Days: Celebrating Jewish Festivals in Poetry and Art.* Garden City, NY: Doubleday & Company, Inc., 1980.

Sachar, Howard M. *A History of Israel: From the Rise of Zionism to Our Time.* New York: Alfred A. Knopf, Inc., 1982.

Silverman, Morris, comp. *High Holiday Prayer Book.* Hartford: Prayer Book Press, 1951.

Strassfeld, Michael. *The Jewish Holidays: A Guide and Commentary.* New York: Harper & Row, Publishers, 1985.

Unger, Merrill F. *Unger's Bible Dictionary.* 3rd ed. Chicago: Moody Press, 1985.

Wiesel, Elie. *Night.* New York: Avon Books, 1969.

Wigoder, Geoffrey, ed. *Encyclopedic Dictionary of Judaica.* Jerusalem. Ketei Publishing House Jerusalem Ltd., 1974.

Wolfson, Ron. *The Art of Jewish Living: Hanukkah.* New York: The Federation of Jewish Men's Clubs, 1990.

Zeitlin, Solomon. *Studies in the Early History of Judaism.* 3 vols. New York: Ktav Publishing House, Inc., 1973.

MORE BOOKS FROM THE FRIENDS OF ISRAEL

by Elwood McQuaid

THE ZION CONNECTON

Elwood McQuaid takes a thoughtful, sensitive look at relations between Jewish people and evangelical Christians, including the controversial issues of anti-Semitism, the rise of Islam, the right of Jewry to a homeland in the Middle East, and whether Christians should try to reach Jewish people with the gospel message—and how.
ISBN-10 0-915540-40-1, #B61
ISBN-13 978-0-915540-40-2

II PETER: STANDING FAST IN THE LAST DAYS

- How can we live for God during these climatic days before the Lord returns?
- How can we identify false teachers and charlatans?
- How can we understand what eternity holds?

This excellent volume provides answers to these important questions from the little but powerful Bible book of 2 Peter. Its timely message will become an invaluable addition to your life as well as your personal library.
ISBN-10 0-915540-65-7, #B79
ISBN-13 978-0-915540-65-5

ZVI: THE MIRACULOUS STORY OF TRIUMPH OVER THE HOLOCAUST

For more than half a century, *ZVI* has endured as the best-selling book produced by the ministry of The Friends of Israel. Millions of people have been touched, inspired, and encouraged by this story of a World War II waif in Warsaw, Poland, and how he found his way to Israel and faith in the Messiah. Now *ZVI* and its sequel, *ZVI and the Next Generation*, are combined in this new release. The whole story—together at last. It is a book you will find difficult to lay down.

ISBN-10 0-915540-66-5, #B80
ISBN-13 978-0-915540-66-2

THE OUTPOURING

Jesus in the Feasts of Israel

This superb book will immeasurably enhance your understanding of how the God certified the credentials of the Jewish Messiah among Abraham's seed in connection with the great, festive commemorations of the Jewish nation. John's Gospel will come alive as you discover the magnificent relationship between the feasts of Israel and the Lord Jesus Christ. *Also available in Russian.*

ISBN-10 0-915540-49-5, #B35, B35R RUSSIAN
ISBN-13 978-0-915540-49-5

by David M. Levy

GUARDING THE GOSPEL OF GRACE

We often lack peace, joy, or victory in our walk with Christ because we're not clear how God's grace works in our lives. The books of Galatians and Jude are brought together in this marvelous work that explains grace and what can happen if you stray from it. Don't miss out on the difference that God's grace can make in your life . . . It's nothing less than amazing!

ISBN-10 0-915540-26-6, #B67
ISBN-13 978-0-915540-26-6

THE TABERNACLE: SHADOWS OF THE MESSIAH

This superb work on Israel's wilderness Tabernacle explores in depth the service of the priesthood and the significance of the sacrifices. The well-organized content and numerous illustraions will open new vistas of biblical truth as ceremonies, sacrifices, and priestly service reveal the perfections of the Messiah

ISBN-10 0-915540-17-7, #B51
ISBN-13 978-0-915540-17-4

REVELATION: HEARING THE LAST WORD

Why is there so much uncertainty and disagreement about the last days? What can we know about the Antichrist? In what order will the events of the last days take place? What will happen to Israel during the Tribulation? What will life be like during the Millennial Kingdom? This valuable resource will help you know what we can expect as we approach earth's final hour

ISBN-10 0-915540-60-6, #B75
ISBN-13 978- 0-915540-60-0

by Renald E. Showers

THOSE INVISIBLE SPIRITS CALLED ANGELS

Everywhere we look, angels are in the spotlight—on prime-time TV, in bestselling books, and on the shelves of well-known gift stores. More and more people report fascinating encounters with angels. But very little of what we're hearing these days matches what the Bible says about angels. And the Bible has a lot to say about who angels are, what they do, and how they minister to us. You'll discover all that and much more in this excellent and easy-to-read volume by Dr. Showers.

ISBN-10 0-915540-24-X, #B66
ISBN-13 978-0-915540-24-2

THERE REALLY IS A DIFFERENCE!

A Comparison of Covenant and Dispensational Theology
Should you attend a church that teaches Covenant Theology or one that teaches Dispensational Theology? Is there a difference between the two? Yes, there is. This excellent volume will explain what these differences are and how they affect issues such as God's ultimate purpose for history, God's program for Israel, the nature and beginning of the church, and the Christian's relationship to the Mosaic Law and grace. It also explores the differences between the premillennial, amillennial, and postmillennial views of the Kingdom of God and presents and apology for the dispensational-premillennial system of theology.
ISBN-10 0-915540-50-9, #B36
ISBN-13 978-0-915540-50-1

MARANATHA: OUR LORD, COME!

A Definitive Study of the Rapture of the Church
Here is an in-depth study of matters related to the Rapture of the church. It addresses such issues as the birth-pang concept in the Bible and ancient Judaism, the biblical concept of the Day of the Lord, the relationship of the Day of the Lord to the Time of Jacob's Trouble and the Great Tribulation, the identification of the sealed scroll of Revelation 5, the significance of the seals, the imminent coming of Christ with His holy angels, the relationship of church saints to the wrath of God, the significance of 2 Thessalonians 2, the implications of both the 70-week prophecy of Daniel 9 and the references to Israel and the church in the book of the Revelation, the meaning of the last trump, and why the timing of the Rapture has practical implications for daily living and ministry.
ISBN-10 0-915540-22-3 #B55P
ISBN-13 978-0-915540-22-8

PASSOVER HAGGADAH

You'll never view communion the same way again after you've read our Passover Haggadah. This beautifully illustrated Haggadah, complete with Heberw songs and prayers, will help you understand the rich symbolism of this important Jewish holiday in light of the sacrifice of Christ, the Lamb of God. And its easy-to-follow format is ideal for helping you conduct your own seder at home, at school, or in church.

ISBN-10 0-915540-69-X, #B29
ISBN-13 978-0-915540-69-3

JEWISH CULTURE & CUSTOMS
A Sampler of Jewish Life
by Steve Herzig

Every area of Jewish life radiates with rich symbolism and special meaning. From meals, clothing, and figures of speech to worship, holidays, and weddings, we find hundreds of fascinating traditions that date as far back as two or three thousand years. How did these customs get started? What special meaning do they hold? And, what can they teach us? Explore the answers to these questions in this enjoyable sampler of the colorful world of Judaism and Jewish life. You'll gain a greater appreciation for God's Chosen People and see key aspects of the Bible and Christianity in a whole new light.

ISBN-10 0-915540-31-2, #B68
ISBN-13 978-0-915540-31-0

ISAIAH'S MESSIAH
by Victor Buksbazen

From the matchless pen of Victor Buksbazen comes an outstanding work on a premier section of the Hebrew Scriptures, Isaiah52—53. This superb little volume masterfully tackles the all-important Jewish question, Of whom did the prophet speak? Of Israel, as most rabbis teach, or of Messiah?

ISBN-10 0-915540-75-4, #B87
ISBN-13 978-0-915540-75-4

The Finest, Most Comprehensive, Biblical History of Israel on DVD

THE PROMISE SERIES

This fantastic, one-of-a-kind series will take you on an exciting tour through the history of the Jewish people—past, present, and future.

With Elwood McQuaid as your personal guide, you'll:

- See actual documentary footage of key events in Israel's past.
- Hear interviews with key people.
- Enjoy exciting views of the land, filmed on location.
- Understand Israel's place in God's program.
- Learn God's Word.
- Appreciate how God is keeping His promises and setting the stage for the future.

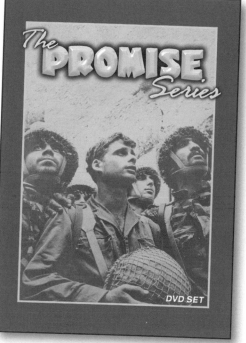

This series is particularly excellent for Bible studies and Sunday schools.

V20D, 3-disc set, UPC 8-24549-2004-3-7
Approx. 4 hours and 15 minutes.